REVISE AQA GCSE (9–1)
Physical Education
REVISION GUIDE

Series Consultant: Harry Smith

Author: Jan Simister

Also available to support your revision:

Revise GCSE Study Skills Guide   9781292318875

The **Revise GCSE Study Skills Guide** is full of tried-and-trusted hints and tips for how to learn more effectively. It gives you techniques to help you achieve your best – throughout your GCSE studies and beyond!

Revise GCSE Revision Planner   9781292318868

The **Revise GCSE Revision Planner** helps you to plan and organise your time, step-by-step, throughout your GCSE revision. Use this book and wall chart to mastermind your revision.

For the full range of Pearson revision titles across KS2, 11+, KS3, GCSE, Functional Skills, AS/A Level and BTEC visit:
www.pearsonschools.co.uk/revise

Question difficulty
Look at this scale next to each exam-style question. It tells you how difficult the question is.

Contents

. . . .

A small bit of small print:
Pearson publishes Sample Assessment Material and the Specification on its website. This is the official content and this book should be used in conjunction with it. The questions and revision tasks in this book have been written to help you revise the skills you may need for your assessment. Remember: the real assessment may not look like this.

Many of the key terms used in this book are explained in a subject-specific vocabulary on page 118.

Bones of the skeleton

The **skeleton** is made up of many bones. Make sure you know the names of the bones at these locations: head/neck, shoulder, chest, elbow, hip, knee and ankle, and that you can recognise these bones on a variety of diagrams.

Front view of upper skeleton

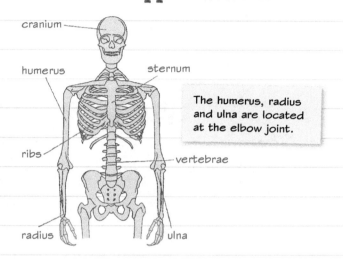

cranium, humerus, sternum, ribs, vertebrae, radius, ulna

The humerus, radius and ulna are located at the elbow joint.

Rear view of upper skeleton

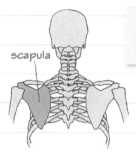

scapula

The humerus and the scapula are located at the shoulder joint.

Golden rule

A good way to remember the names and locations of the bones is to practise by labelling blank diagrams of the skeleton.

Front view of lower skeleton

- The pelvis and femur are located at the hip joint.
- The femur and the tibia meet at the knee joint and the patella sits in front of the joint.
- The tibia, fibula and talus are located at the ankle joint.

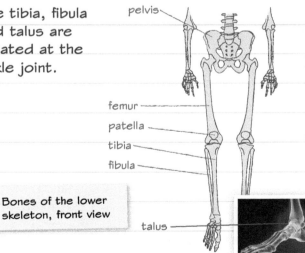

pelvis, femur, patella, tibia, fibula, talus

Bones of the lower skeleton, front view

Worked example

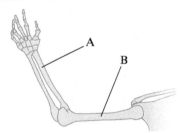

A
B

Identify the bones at A and B.　**(2 marks)**

A: Radius
B: Humerus

Sometimes it is hard to remember which bone is the radius and which is the ulna. Remember: the radius is the bone that is near the thumb.

Now try this

Figure 1

The knee joint makes it possible for the rugby player to run during the game.
State **two** bones located at the knee joint that allow the player in **Figure 1** to run.
(2 marks)

Structure of the skeleton

We classify bones by their shape. Each bone type or classification has a particular function. You need to know the classification type of each bone and its function, and to be able to explain the use of each in physical activity.

Identifying bones

The skeleton:

 provides a framework for muscle attachment

 works together with the muscular system to enable movement at joints.

When muscles contract they pull on the bone, creating movement.

> A joint is a place where two or more bones meet. Different types of joints allow different types of movements.

The shape and type of the bone determines the amount of movement that occurs at each joint.

> Remember to look at the shape of the bone, to help identify what type of bone it is.

Long bones

Long bones enable gross movement by working as levers.

Examples of long bones are:

• the humerus

• the femur.

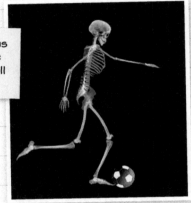

> Long bones work as a lever to increase the pace of the ball when kicked.

Short bones

Short bones:

 are as wide as they are long

 allow finer, controlled movements.

Examples of short bones include:

• the carpals (in the wrist)

• the tarsals (in the ankle).

Flat bones

Flat bones provide protection of vital organs and a broad surface for muscles to attach to.

Examples of flat bones include:

• the cranium   • the ribs   • the scapula.

Example of use:

• The cranium protects the brain if hit by a cricket ball.

Worked example

Which **type** of bone is the ulna?   **(1 mark)**

A Flat bone   ○
B Long bone   ●
C Irregular bone   ○
D Short bone   ○

> If you are not sure, think about where the ulna is. Then think: does it look similar to any bones you know the classification of? Remember that bones are classified by shape; so if it is the same shape as a bone you **do** know, go for that option.

Now try this

> Make sure you identify the bone type you are explaining.

Figure 1

Explain how the bone type at the cranium makes it possible for the player in **Figure 1** to head the ball.   **(3 marks)**

Functions of the skeleton

You need to know the functions of the skeleton and how they apply to physical activity and sport.

Key functions

The functions of the skeleton are:

- support
- production of blood cells
- storage of minerals
- protection of vital organs
- structural shape and muscle attachment
- formation of joints for movement.

You need to be able to explain how the skeleton carries out all of these functions by giving examples of each in relation to physical activity.

Blood cell production

The following types of blood cell are produced in bone marrow. They are all beneficial to physical performance.

- Platelets help clotting if you are cut.
- Red blood cells transport oxygen to working muscles.
- White blood cells help fight infection.

Mineral storage

Calcium and phosphorus are stored in bones to help strengthen them.

Support

Your skeleton provides support by providing a structural shape for muscles and tissues to attach to. This keeps the muscles in place and gives you your shape.

Protection

Your skeleton provides protection for your vital organs, including the heart.

For example, your skull protects your brain if an opponent follows through wildly with their hockey stick and it hits you on the head during a game.

Aid to movement

- The bones provide a place for the muscles to **attach** to, so that when the muscles contract they **pull** the bones to cause movement. Movement occurs at the **joints** of the skeleton.
- Bones also act as **levers**. Levers allow the body to increase the force it can generate or increase the speed of the movement. For example, a tennis player with longer levers will generate more force on a serve.

Worked example

Which of the following options is correct to complete the sentence below?   **(1 mark)**
The skeletal system protects:
A vital organs, for example, bones, muscles, tendons
B by providing a hard structure over the organ needing protection
C by providing a structure for support
D by producing red blood cells which fight disease

Now try this

The skeletal system has several functions. Describe how the skeleton aids movement.   **(2 marks)**

3

Structure of a synovial joint

You need to be able to identify the structures that make up a **synovial joint**. You also need to explain the function of each of these structures and how they help to prevent injury.

Components of a synovial joint

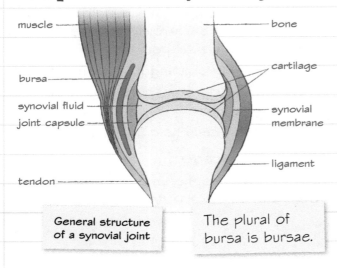

muscle
bone
cartilage
bursa
synovial fluid
synovial membrane
joint capsule
ligament
tendon

General structure of a synovial joint

The plural of bursa is bursae.

Function of each component

Cartilage is a shiny, elastic material that:
👍 reduces friction
👍 absorbs shock.

Ligaments connect bone to bone and stabilise the joint, holding the bones in the correct position.

The **joint capsule** surrounds the synovial joint. It is attached to the outer layer of the bones forming the joint. It:
👍 seals the joint
👍 provides stability to the joint.

The **synovial membrane** secretes synovial fluid.

Synovial fluid:
👍 lubricates and reduces friction in the joint
👍 supplies nutrients to the joint
👍 removes waste products from the joint.

Bursae are in most major synovial joints. They:
👍 reduce mechanical friction in the joint
👍 act as a cushion between the bone and another part of the joint, such as the tendons or muscles.

Summary of injury prevention

The components of a synovial joint:
✓ reduce any shock on a joint that can occur during physical activity, by cushioning the joint.

The joint lubrication helps to prevent injury during physical activity by:
✓ helping to prevent friction, that is the rubbing together of parts of the joint causing wear and tear
✓ supporting the removal of tiny particles of waste that could otherwise cause damage to the joint.

Think about the function of the structure labelled A. What is its job? Then think how this structure helps to prevent injury.

Worked example

1 (a) Identify the structure labelled A.   **(1 mark)**
Synovial fluid

(b) Explain how this structure helps to prevent injury.   **(2 marks)**
The synovial fluid reduces friction in the joint and therefore stops the wear and tear on the performer's cartilage.

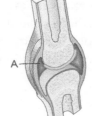

A

Now try this

How would the bursae aid sporting performance in contact activities such as wrestling or judo?   **(3 marks)**

Types of freely movable joints

You need to be able to identify two types of freely moveable joints at their various locations in the body. You also need to know the bones located at each of these joints.

Pages 5–8 contain the content for **3.1.2.1: Analysis of basic movements in sporting examples.**

About joints

- A joint is the place where two or more bones meet. It is where movement can occur.
- Although there are many joints in the human body, you only need to know the joints on this page.
- You should be able to see the similarities between the same types of joints.
- You should be able to give sporting examples of the use of each joint.

Golden rule

Remember it is the formation of the joint that dictates the type of movement that can occur there.

Hinge joints

Located at the:

- knee
- elbow
- ankle.

Movement at hinge joints:

- flexion
- extension

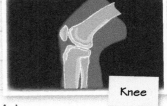
Knee

Ball and socket joints

Located at the:

- hip
- shoulder.

Movement at ball and socket joints:

- flexion
- extension
- rotation
- abduction
- adduction

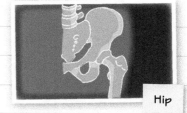
Hip

Identification of joints

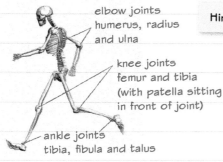

elbow joints
humerus, radius and ulna

Hinge joints

knee joints
femur and tibia
(with patella sitting in front of joint)

ankle joints
tibia, fibula and talus

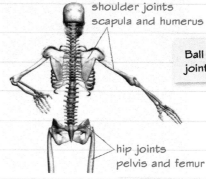

shoulder joints
scapula and humerus

Ball and socket joints

hip joints
pelvis and femur

If you are not sure, use your own body to try to work it out.

Identify the type of movement possible at **both** hinge and ball and socket joints. **(1 mark)**

A Adduction ☐   C Flexion ●
B Rotation ☐   D Abduction ☐

Now try this

What type of joint is formed at the shoulder? **(1 mark)**

A Ball and socket ☐   C Dovetail ☐
B Ball joint ☐   D Hinge ☐

Movement at joints 1

You need to know the different types of movement that are linked to the joint types and be able to apply these movements to specific sporting actions. Pages 5–8 contain the content for 3.1.2.1: Analysis of basic movements in sporting examples.

Joint action: flexion

Flexion is the term given when the angle at a joint **decreases**.

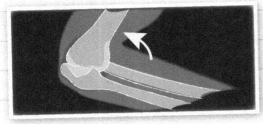

This happens when the bones forming the joint move closer together.

Joint type and application

Flexion occurs at hinge and ball and socket joints.

For example, it occurs at the knee when the player is preparing to kick a football.

The lower part of your leg gets closer to the upper part of your leg as the angle at the joint decreases.

Joint action: extension

Extension is the term given when the angle at a joint **increases**.

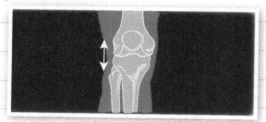

This happens when the bones forming the joint move away from each other.

> Flexion and extension occur at the shoulder, elbow, hip and knee.

Joint type and application

Extension occurs at hinge and ball and socket joints.

For example, it occurs at the knee when following through after kicking a football.

The lower part of your leg gets further away from the upper part of your leg as the angle at the joint increases.

Worked example

State the main range of movement possible at the knee joint. **(1 mark)**

The range of movement at the knee joint is flexion to extension.

Flexion and extension could be written in any order but you do need to include both. If a question asks for the range of movement at a joint, you need to put down both parts because the range is the whole movement covered.

Now try this

Identify the joint action necessary to bend the batting (right) arm at the elbow to move into the position shown in **Figure 1**. **(1 mark)**

Figure 1

This question asks for the joint action. Watch out for the different terms and make sure you are not confusing joint action with joint type or muscle action.

Movement at joints 2

This page covers the joint actions of abduction, adduction and rotation, which occur at ball and socket joints. Knowledge of these joint actions will allow you to analyse basic movements in sport. Pages 5–8 contain the content for **3.1.2.1: Analysis of basic movements in sporting examples.**

Joint actions

Abduction = the movement of a limb **away** from the midline of the body

Adduction = the movement of a limb towards the midline of the body

Rotation = when the bone at a joint moves around its own **axis**, so making a circular movement

Rotation allows for the biggest range of movement, for example, from when the fingers enter the water all the way round until they enter the water again.

Joint type and application

Abduction occurs at ball and socket joints (hip and shoulder).

For example, there is abduction at the shoulder when reaching out sideways to intercept a netball.

To help you remember:
If something is 'abducted', it is taken away.

Adduction occurs at ball and socket joints (hip and shoulder).

For example, adduction occurs at the hip in the cross-over leg action when throwing a javelin. The leg comes back towards the midline of the body.

To help you remember:
Adduction starts with 'add', so it is when a limb is added to the midline of the body.

Rotation occurs at ball and socket joints (hip and shoulder).

For example, it occurs at the shoulder when swimming front crawl. The arm rotates around in a circular motion.

Worked example

Use the image as a guide – it will have been included to help you.

Which of the following is the correct term for the joint action that occurs when the ski jumper takes their arms away from the midline of the body to achieve the position shown in **Figure 1**? **(1 mark)**

A Abduction ●
B Adduction ○
C Flexion ○
D Extension ○

Figure 1

Now try this

The word 'range' means you need to include both the start and finish movement for the action identified.

Identify the range of movement at the shoulder during a star jump. **(1 mark)**

Movement at joints 3

In addition to the joint actions on pages 6–7, there are two other joint actions you need to know: plantar flexion and dorsiflexion. These movements only occur at the hinge joint at the ankle. Pages 5–8 contain the content for **3.1.2.1: Analysis of basic movements in sporting examples.**

Joint action: plantar flexion

- Occurs at the ankle joint.
- Movement of the foot downwards away from the front of the ankle.

For example, plantar flexion occurs when:

- kicking a football with the laces of a boot
- a gymnast points their toes.

Plantar flexion of the ankle occurs as the gymnast points her toes to make the shape more aesthetically pleasing.

Joint action: dorsiflexion

- Occurs at the ankle joint.
- Movement of the foot upwards towards the shin (decreasing the angle at the joint).

Dorsiflexion occurs at the ankle of the leading leg as the athlete jumps the hurdle.

State the name of the joint type where plantar flexion takes place and give an example of its use. **(2 marks)**

Hinge joint. Pointing the toes so you can kick a football with the laces of the boot.

Make sure you read the question carefully. This question is asking for the name of a **joint type**, not the name of a **joint**.

Golden rule

Always try to apply your answers to examples in physical activity.

Briefly explain how the joint action at the ankle in **Figure 1** shown assists the volleyball player in their sport. **(2 marks)**

The joint action has not been named, so it would be a good idea to name it and then explain how it might help.

Figure 1

Muscles

You need to know the role of tendons and the names of the muscles identified on pages 9–13, as well as being able to recognise these muscles on a variety of diagrams. These muscles are attached to the bones located at the joints identified on page 5. Turn to page 1 for more on bones and page 5 for more on joints.

Muscles of the shoulder and back

Name: **Deltoid**

Location: Top of the shoulder

Role: Abducts the arm at the shoulder

Example: Lifting your arms above your head to block the ball in volleyball

Name: **Rotator cuffs**

Location: On the scapula in the shoulder

Role: Rotation of shoulder

Example: Bowling in cricket

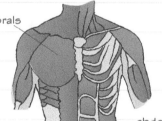

deltiod

latissimus dorsi

rotator cuffs

Name: **Latissimus dorsi**

Location: Side of back

Role: Adducts the upper arm at the shoulder / rotates the humerus

Example: Bringing arms back to side during a straight jump in trampolining

The deltoids and latissimus dorsi work as an **antagonistic pair** to raise and lower the arm at the shoulder. Antagonistic pairs are explained on page 10.

Muscles of the chest and abdomen

Name: **Pectorals**

Location: Front of upper chest

Role: Adducts the arm at the shoulder

Example: Follow-through from a forehand drive in tennis

pectorals

abdominals

Name: **Abdominals**

Location: Front of body between pelvis and ribs

Role: Flexion of trunk

Example: Sit-ups

Which one of the following muscles is contracting to allow the tennis player in **Figure 1** to adduct his arm at the shoulder?

(1 mark)

A Triceps ○
B Latissimus dorsi ○
C Abdominals ○
D Pectorals ●

Figure 1

Tendons

The role of the tendons is to join (skeletal) **muscle to bone**. Tendons are formed of a tough connective tissue.

Tendons are relevant to sport and physical activity because they hold the muscle to the bone – when the muscle contracts it pulls on the bone causing movement at joints.

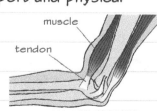

muscle

tendon

Tendons join muscles to bones.

Name the movement that occurs when the deltoids contract **and** give an example of its use in a physical activity of your choice.

(2 marks)

Antagonistic pairs: biceps and triceps

Antagonistic pairs of muscles create opposing movement at joints. You need to know the **four** different pairs covered on the following pages and relate them to sporting techniques.

Antagonistic pairs

Skeletal muscles work together to provide movement of the joints.

While one muscle **contracts**, another **relaxes** to create movement.

Muscles working together like this are called **antagonistic pairs**.

The muscle contracting is the **agonist** (prime mover).

The muscle relaxing is the **antagonist**.

Remember, muscles are connected to bones via tendons. When the muscles contract, they pull on the tendon which pulls on the bone. This creates the movement.

Biceps and triceps

These two muscles are an example of an antagonistic muscle pair.

Name: **Biceps**

Location: Front of upper arm

Role: Flexion of the arm at the elbow

Example: Upwards phase of a biceps curl

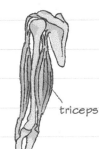
biceps

triceps

Name: **Triceps**

Location: Back of upper arm

Role: Extension of the arm at the elbow

Example: Straightening the arms in a chest press

During this part of the movement, the triceps is the antagonist – it is relaxing to allow the biceps to contract.

During this movement, the biceps is the antagonist – it is relaxing to allow the triceps to contract.

Worked example

Explain the term 'antagonistic pair' in relation to muscle movement.   **(1 mark)**

One muscle contracts while the other relaxes to bring about movement.

EXAM ALERT!

Explain the role of **each** muscle in the antagonistic pair.

Now try this

Complete the blanks by identifying the muscles involved in the movement described, as shown in **Figure 1**.   **(2 marks)**

The .... is the agonist when the goalkeeper extends her arm at the elbow and the .... is the antagonist.

Figure 1

Antagonistic pairs: quadriceps and hamstrings

You need to know which muscles work together to bring about movement and use this knowledge to analyse sporting actions.

The quadriceps and hamstrings are an antagonistic muscle pair.

Name: **Quadriceps**
Location: Front of upper leg
Role: Extension of the leg at the knee
Example: Straightening the leading leg going over a hurdle

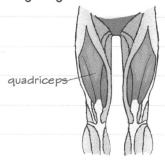

During this part of the movement the hamstrings act as the antagonist. They are relaxing to allow the quadriceps to contract.

Name: **Hamstrings**
Location: Back of upper leg
Role: Flexion of the leg at the knee
Example: Bending the trailing leg going over a hurdle

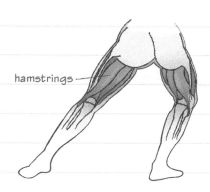

During this part of the movement the quadriceps is the antagonist. It is relaxing to allow the hamstrings to contract.

The quadriceps and hamstrings work together so the performer can clear the hurdle.

Golden rules
- ☑ If you are not sure of the correct spelling of muscle names, write them like they sound.
- ☑ Always write the name in full, for example, quadriceps, not quads.

Worked example

Which one of the following muscles is contracting to allow the cyclist in **Figure 1** to flex her leg at the knee?   **(1 mark)**

A Latissimus dorsi ⊘   ☐ C Gastrocnemius ⊘
B Hamstrings ●   ☐ D Quadriceps ⊘

Figure 1

EXAM ALERT!

Make sure you know the actions of the muscles. Questions often have a picture to help you visualise the movement.

Now try this

Name the antagonist that is relaxing to allow the cyclist in the image above to flex her leg at the knee.   **(1 mark)**

Antagonistic pairs: gastrocnemius and tibialis anterior

Make sure you know the names and locations of these muscles and can give an example of their use.

Name: **Gastrocnemius**

Location: Back of lower leg

Role: Plantar flexion at the ankle

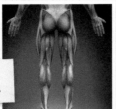

The **gastrocnemius** muscles are highlighted.

Name: **Tibialis anterior**

Location: Front of lower leg

Role: Dorsiflexion at the ankle

The **tibialis anterior** muscles are highlighted.

Example: Pointing the toes when performing a pike jump in trampolining

Example: Bringing the toes up towards the shins when extending the legs in the long jump

Golden rule

Always use the correct name for the gastrocnemius, not the calf. Also remember it has a 'C' sound in it (gast-ro-C-nemius).

Which action is plantar flexion?

To help you recall which action is plantar flexion, remember:

Pointing toes starts with the letter **P** and so does the action **p**lantar flexion.

Where is the tibialis anterior?

To help you recall where the tibialis anterior muscle is located, remember:

- the word 'anterior' means front
- the word 'tibialis' starts with the name of the bone – the tibia
- the muscle is located on the front of the tibia.

Worked example

What term is being described below? **(1 mark)**
When two muscles work together, one muscle starts to contract to pull the bone, the other starts to relax to aid the movement.

Antagonistic pair

Golden rule

When asked to give an example, always use the most obvious example to make sure it is correct, rather than giving a more obscure answer.

Now try this

Double check whether a question is asking for the agonist or the antagonist.

Figure 1

Name the antagonist supporting the agonist to allow the gymnast in **Figure 1** to point his toes. **(1 mark)**

Antagonistic pairs: hip flexors and gluteals

Make sure you know the names and locations of these muscles and can give an example of their use.

Name: **Hip flexors**

Location: Very top of front of upper leg

Role: Flexion of leg at the hip

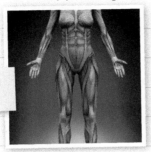

The **hip flexor** muscles are highlighted.

Name: **Gluteals**

Location: Buttocks

Role: Extension of the leg at the hip

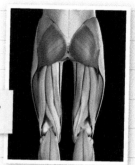

The **gluteals** muscles are highlighted.

Example: Bringing the legs up in a seat-drop in trampolining

Example: Lifting the leg back at the hip when running

Example of hip flexion in diving

Golden rules

Notice the words **flexion** and **extension** are used for the action at the hip as well as the knee. The same rules apply.

✓ Flexion occurs when the angle at the joint gets smaller.

✓ Extension occurs when the angle at the joint gets bigger.

Example of hip extension in basketball

Worked example

Note that the question refers to the hip, not the knee, and asks about extension rather than flexion.

Which **one** of the following muscles is contracting to allow the footballer in **Figure 1** to extend her leg at the hip? **(1 mark)**

A Gluteals   ⬤   C Abdominals   ◯

B Hamstrings   ◯   D Quadriceps   ◯

Figure 1

Now try this

Name the agonist that brings the thighs up to the chest in a tuck jump and identify the joint action occurring at the hip. **(2 marks)**

Muscle contractions

You need to know the different types of muscle contraction – **isotonic** and **isometric** – as well as the difference between concentric and eccentric isotonic muscle contractions.

Any physical activity requires movement. All movement is achieved through working the muscles by contracting them. The muscles also need to work to hold the body in a stationary pose.

Muscle contraction

There are two different types of muscle contraction, used for different purposes. You need to know the terms for them and be able to explain the two types.

- **Isotonic** muscle contractions are those that result in movement.
- **Isometric** muscle contractions are where the muscles contract but there is no visible movement.

Always use a stationary example for isometric contractions, and include the word 'stationary'. For example: 'The stationary phase of a rugby scrum is an example of an isometric muscle contraction.'

Examples of muscle contractions

Isotonic contractions provide movement of the limbs.

Isometric contractions hold the whole body in balance and there is no movement.

The difference between concentric and eccentric isotonic contractions

During **isotonic** muscle contractions the type of contraction is either concentric or eccentric.

- **Concentric muscle contraction** is when the muscle shortens during the contraction. Example: biceps muscle contracting to lift a weight during a biceps curl activity.
- **Eccentric muscle contraction** is when the muscle lengthens during the contraction. Example: biceps muscle contracting to lower and control the weight during a biceps curl activity.

the biceps muscle shortens as the weight is raised

the biceps muscle lengthens as the weight is lowered

Concentric and eccentric muscle contractions during the upward and downward phases of a biceps curl

Worked example

The gymnast in **Figure 1** is holding a position on the rings. What type of muscle contraction is taking place to allow the gymnast to hold this position? **(2 marks)**

Isometric muscle contraction

Figure 1

Now try this

Using an example, describe the difference between eccentric and concentric muscle contractions. **(3 marks)**

The pathway of air

You need to be able to identify several of the structures used in the pathway of air from outside the body to the **alveoli** in the lungs. The actual mechanics of breathing is covered on page 21.

The pathway of air

- Enters the body through the **mouth** and **nose**.
- Then travels down through the **trachea** to the **lungs**.

The trachea

Rings of cartilage surround the trachea. These help the trachea to keep its shape and prevent collapse, so allowing the air to pass through to the lungs.

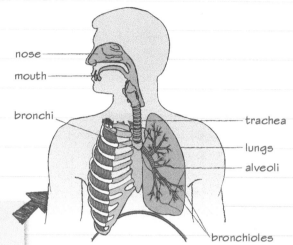

nose
mouth
bronchi
trachea
lungs
alveoli
bronchioles

Structures used in pathway of air

Lungs

- There are two lungs (left and right).
- The lungs allow the movement of air in and out of the body (ventilation).
- Air enters the lungs during inspiration (the process of breathing in).
- Air leaves the lungs during expiration (the process of breathing out).

Bronchi and bronchioles

- The air travels to each of the lungs via the **bronchi** – the term for both the left and right bronchus that take air to each of the lungs.
- The passages that the air travels down get smaller as the bronchi subdivide. The smaller airways from the bronchi are called **bronchioles**.
- Bronchioles branch out throughout the lungs and carry the air from the bronchi to the **alveoli**.

Worked example

Which one of these describes the correct pathway of air? **(1 mark)**

A mouth; nose; trachea; bronchioles; alveoli; lungs ◯

B nose; mouth; lungs; trachea; bronchi; alveoli ◯

C mouth; trachea; bronchi; alveoli; bronchioles; lungs ◯

D nose; trachea; bronchi; lungs; bronchioles; alveoli ●

Discount the clearly incorrect responses first. Diffusion of oxygen from air takes place in the alveoli. This means the alveoli must be the final part of the pathway, so the answer must be either B or D.

Alveoli

- The alveoli are tiny air sacs.
- They are attached to the branches of the bronchioles throughout the lungs.
- At the alveoli the exchange of oxygen and carbon dioxide occurs.

See page 16 for more on the alveoli.

There are millions of alveoli in the lungs.

Now try this

Describe the pathway of air through the respiratory system from the trachea to the alveoli. **(3 marks)**

Gaseous exchange

You need to know the features that assist with gaseous exchange, including the structure of the alveoli, and how the gases are transported within the blood.

Gaseous exchange

Gases always move from high to low areas of concentration.

- Oxygen diffuses into the bloodstream from the alveoli in the lungs.
- The oxygen then binds (joins) with the **haemoglobin** in the red blood cells, to form oxyhaemoglobin.
- Oxyhaemoglobin is transported to the working muscles, where it is needed for aerobic activity.
- Carbon dioxide produced in the tissue is transported away from the muscles by the haemoglobin.

Golden rule

Remember: gaseous exchange is the exchange of one gas for another gas. It is NOT turning one gas into another.

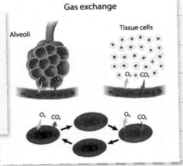

Gas exchange occurs between the alveoli and the capillaries, and between the capillaries and the muscle tissue.

Gas exchange

Alveoli   Tissue cells

Features that assist in gaseous exchange

- The alveoli are tiny air sacs with moist, thin walls (only one-cell thick).
- The combined surface area of the alveoli is very large, allowing plenty of opportunity for gases to pass through.
- There are lots of capillaries very close to the alveoli, so there is only a short distance for the gases to diffuse through (short diffusion pathway) and a large blood supply.

Gas exchange – alveoli to capillaries

- The alveoli have a high oxygen concentration.
- The capillaries surrounding the alveoli have a low concentration of oxygen.
- Oxygen moves from high concentration to low, through the thin walls of the alveoli and capillaries. In this way the capillaries gain oxygen to transport around the body.

Gas exchange – capillaries to alveoli

The reverse happens with the movement of carbon dioxide.

- Capillaries surrounding the alveoli have a high pressure/concentration of CO_2 (from muscles).
- Alveoli have a low pressure/concentration of CO_2.
- Movement of CO_2 from high pressure to low.
- CO_2 is moved out of the blood into the alveoli to be breathed out.

Exercise intensities

Gas exchange varies with the intensity of exercise.

 During aerobic activity there is an increase in breathing rate and an increase in gas exchange to meet the demands of the working muscles for more oxygen.

 After anaerobic activity there is an elevated breathing rate, allowing greater gas exchange to aid recovery.

Worked example

Explain one reason why carbon dioxide can diffuse from a capillary to the alveoli. **(2 marks)**

There will be high levels of carbon dioxide in the capillaries and lower levels in the alveoli, therefore the carbon dioxide will move from high pressure in the capillaries to the alveoli to try to even out the concentration of CO_2.

Now try this

(a) What will the concentration of oxygen in the blood be just after it leaves the alveoli?

(b) Give a reason for your answer to (a).   **(2 marks)**

Blood vessels

You need to know both the structure and function of the blood vessels and how this is relevant in terms of **blood pressure**, carrying oxygenated blood and deoxygenated blood, and gas exchange. Turn to page 16 for more on gaseous exchange, for more on the redistribution of blood during exercise turn to page 18, revise the names of the arteries and veins around the heart on page 19.

Arteries

Structure

- Thick muscular and elastic walls
- Small internal diameter (lumen)

Functions

- Carry blood at high pressure **away** from the heart
- Mainly carry **oxygenated** blood (exception: pulmonary artery carries **deoxygenated** blood to lungs from heart)

Relevance

Blood pressure increases during exercise as the working muscles demand more oxygen, increasing blood flow. The muscles in the artery walls contract and relax automatically. When the muscle relaxes, the arteries dilate so there is more room for the blood to travel through, helping regulate blood pressure.

Capillaries

Structure

- Very thin walls (only one-cell thick)
- Small internal diameter

Functions

- Link smaller arteries with smaller veins
- Carry blood at very low pressure

Relevance

Capillaries allow **gaseous exchange**. Walls are very thin to allow gases and nutrients to pass through them, therefore getting oxygen to the muscles and removing carbon dioxide.

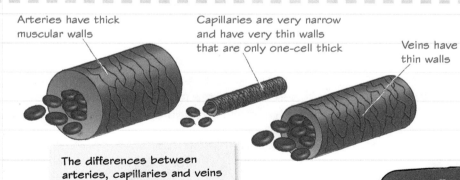

Arteries have thick muscular walls

Capillaries are very narrow and have very thin walls that are only one-cell thick

Veins have thin walls

The differences between arteries, capillaries and veins

Golden rule

Remember: all arteries carry blood **away** from the heart and all veins carry blood **towards** the heart.

Veins

Structure

- Thin walls
- Large internal diameter
- Contain valves

Functions

- Carry blood at low pressure **towards** heart
- Mainly carry **deoxygenated** blood (exception: pulmonary vein carries **oxygenated** blood from lungs to heart)

Relevance

Veins carry deoxygenated blood from the muscles. The wide internal diameter allows blood to pass through more easily and the valves help return the blood to the heart by preventing backflow due to low pressure.

Worked example

Which one of the following is a characteristic of capillaries? **(1 mark)**

A Has valves ⊘
B Thick muscular wall ⊘
C One-cell thick ●
D Carries blood under high pressure ⊘

Think about the function of capillaries. The capillaries need to be thin to allow the gases to move in and out of them easily.

Now try this

State the type of blood vessel that holds blood at high pressure. **(1 mark)**

Redistribution of blood

You need to know the role of the blood vessels in the redistribution of blood during exercise and be able to use the terms **vasoconstriction** and **vasodilation**.

Redistribution of blood flow

When you exercise your working muscles need more oxygen. Oxygen is attached to the red blood cells in the blood and carried to your active muscles.

Your heart rate and stroke volume increase so more blood is circulating every minute. For more on heart rate and stroke volume, turn to page 20.

Blood is diverted away from inactive areas to the working muscles. This is called **redistribution of blood flow**.

Blood can be redistributed away from the stomach. This is why it is important that digestion is complete before exercise begins.

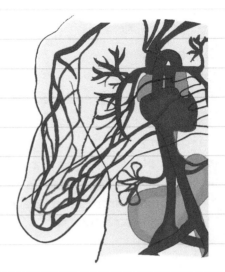

Vasoconstriction

- Vasoconstriction means that the blood vessels are constricted (squeezed) to make them smaller.
- When you start to exercise, chemical changes trigger signals from your nervous system.
- These signals cause the blood vessels that supply the **inactive** areas (for example, the digestive system) to **constrict**, reducing blood flow to these areas.

Vasodilation

- Vasodilation means that the blood vessels are dilated to make them bigger.
- When you start to exercise, chemical changes trigger signals from your nervous system.
- These signals cause the blood vessels that supply the **active** areas (the working muscles) to **dilate**, increasing blood flow to these areas. This means that these muscles receive more oxygen and nutrients.

Worked example

> You could use alternative words to 'greater' and 'lower', such as 'more' or 'less', but always re-read your answer to make sure the meaning is clear.

Using the words in the table below, complete the following statements about blood flow while at rest and during physical activity.

unchanged	equal
lower	greater

Blood flow to the digestive system is ......_greater_...... at rest than when exercising.   **(1 mark)**
Blood flow to the muscular system is ......_lower_...... at rest than when exercising.   **(1 mark)**

Now try this

Using the words in the table below, complete the statements that follow.

redistribution of blood	digestion
cardiac output	increased blood flow

Reduced blood flow to specific areas of the body is achieved through ....
There is a need for .... to the muscles during exercise.   **(2 marks)**

Heart structure and the cardiac cycle

You need to know some of the components that make up the heart and the order of the **cardiac cycle** and pathway of blood, including diastole (filling) and systole (ejection) of the **chambers**.

Structure of the heart

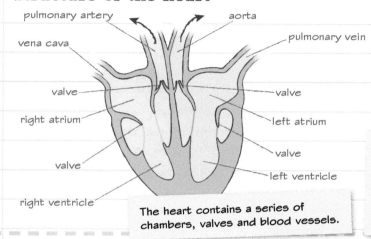

pulmonary artery
vena cava
valve
right atrium
valve
right ventricle

aorta
pulmonary vein
valve
left atrium
valve
left ventricle

The heart contains a series of chambers, valves and blood vessels.

Golden rule

When looking at a diagram of the heart remember that it is a cross-section, viewed from the front. This is why the right-hand side is actually on the left of the diagram! Imagine your heart to check the sides.

Remember: valves help to keep blood moving forward. They open owing to the pressure of the blood. They shut after the blood has passed through, to prevent **backflow** (the blood flowing back again).

The cardiac cycle

The cardiac cycle is the repeated contraction and relaxation of the heart.

When the heart beats, blood passes through the vessels and chambers in a specific order. Both the right side of the heart and the left side contract and relax at the same time.

There are two phases:

* **Diastole** is when the chamber relaxes and fills with blood.
* **Systole** is when the chamber contracts, ejecting the blood within it.

The pathway of blood

* The **right atrium** contracts (systole) ejecting deoxygenated blood through a valve in to the **right ventricle**: the right ventricle relaxes and fills (diastole) with the **deoxygenated blood**.
* The **right ventricle** then contracts (systole) pushing the deoxygenated blood through valves to the **pulmonary artery**.
* The **pulmonary artery** carries deoxygenated blood **away** from the heart to the lungs to receive oxygen via gas exchange.
* The **pulmonary vein** transports **oxygenated blood** from the lungs to the **left atrium**, which relaxes and fills (diastole).
* The left ventricle then contracts (systole) ejecting the oxygenated blood through valves to the **aorta**.
* The **aorta** is the main artery and carries oxygenated blood away from the **left ventricle** to take oxygen to the working muscles.
* The **vena cava** is the main vein bringing deoxygenated blood back to the **right atrium** so it can be pumped to the lungs to collect oxygen.

Worked example

Explain the function of the pulmonary artery.
(2 marks)

The pulmonary artery carries deoxygenated blood from the heart to the lungs so the blood can get oxygen, which is eventually pumped to the working muscles.

Now try this

Complete the diagram to show the missing components assisting the flow of deoxygenated blood to the lungs.
(2 marks)

| vena cava | → | | → | valve | → | right ventricle | → | | → | pulmonary artery |

Cardiac output

You need to know about **cardiac output** and its components (**stroke volume** and **heart rate**). You also need to know how to interpret graphs showing heart rates.

Key terms

Heart rate (HR): the number of times the heart beats per minute.

Stroke volume (SV): the amount of blood ejected from the heart with each beat.

Cardiac output (Q): the amount of blood leaving the heart per minute.

Cardiac output (Q) = SV × HR.

Anticipatory rise: a rise in HR prior to exercise.

Changes in heart rate before and during exercise

Immediately before exercise starts:

- there is an increase in HR (anticipatory rise) due to the release of the hormone **adrenaline**. The body detects this change and increases the HR to increase oxygen delivery in preparation for exercise.

When you start to exercise:

- your muscles demand more oxygen, and the blood transports this oxygen
- to increase delivery of oxygen, cardiac output increases by increasing HR and/or SV.

Interpreting heart rate graphs

A. At rest the HR is at its lowest.

B. Immediately before exercise there is an increase in HR (anticipatory rise).

C. At the start of physical activity, as the intensity increases, there is a sharp increase in heart rate.

D. During continuous exercise the HR levels out.

E. Immediately after exercise there is a sharp drop in HR.

F. HR levels out and is slowly returning to resting HR.

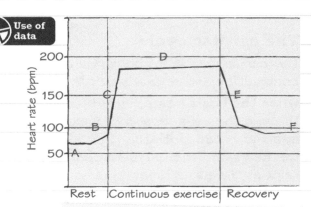

Use of data

Resting, working and recovery heart rates, before, during and after exercise

 Worked example Use of data

Use the information you are given:
HR × SV = cardiac output

Analyse the graph to determine the effect of exercise on cardiac output. **(3 marks)**

The graph shows an increase in heart rate and stroke volume. As heart rate multiplied by stroke volume equals cardiac output, if they have both increased cardiac output must also increase as a result of exercise.

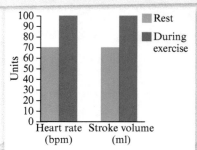

 Now try this ○ Use the information in the graph to guide you.

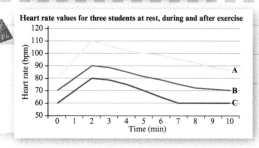

Heart rate values for three students at rest, during and after exercise

(a) Which student had the lowest resting heart rate?

(b) Whose pulse rate increased the most during exercise?

(c) Which student recovered from exercise the quickest? **(3 marks)**

Mechanics of breathing

You need to know the mechanics of breathing (how it works) and the interaction of the intercostal muscles, ribs and diaphragm in this process. When you breathe, you breathe in (inhaling) and out (exhaling), to bring air into and out of the lungs.

Inhaling and exhaling at rest

During **inspiration**:

- the (external) **intercostal** muscles contract, raising the rib cage
- the diaphragm flattens
- the volume in the chest cavity increases, reducing the pressure in the lungs causing the air to rush in.

During forced **expiration** (breathing out a greater volume of air than in a normal breath):

- the (internal) **intercostal** muscles contract, lowering the rib cage
- the diaphragm rises
- the volume in the chest cavity decreases, increasing air pressure in the lungs forcing air out.

The changes in air pressure cause the inhalation and exhalation.

Inhaling and exhaling during exercise

During exercise:

- the mechanics of breathing are the same as at rest
- the breathing rate and depth increases.

During **inspiration**:

- the **pectoral** muscles also pull the rib cage out and **sternocleidomastoid** muscles raise the sternum at the front of the rib cage, allowing the lungs to expand even more.

During **expiration**:

- the rib cage is pulled down quicker, due to the use of the **abdominal** muscles, which forces the air out faster.

Note: you may see the terms 'inspiration' or 'inhalation' for breathing in and 'expiration' or 'exhalation' for breathing out.

Inspiration and expiration

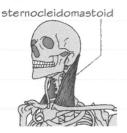
sternocleidomastoid

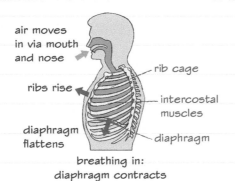
air moves in via mouth and nose
rib cage
ribs rise
intercostal muscles
diaphragm flattens
diaphragm
breathing in: diaphragm contracts

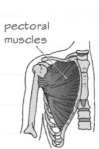
pectoral muscles

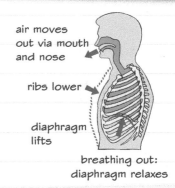
air moves out via mouth and nose
ribs lower
diaphragm lifts
breathing out: diaphragm relaxes

Worked example

The question asks about breathing, so make sure you mention both inhalation and exhalation in your answer.

Explain the role of the pectorals in breathing. **(5 marks)**

The pectorals are located in the chest. When they contract they pull on the rib cage. This expands the rib cage, increasing the size of the chest cavity so the lungs can expand. As the lungs are expanding this means this occurs during inhalation. The pectorals do not assist with exhalation.

Now try this

There are three marks available, so make sure you identify three muscles.

Other than the pectorals, identify the muscles that assist with inhalation during exercise. **(3 marks)**

Lung volumes

You need to be able to identify lung volumes on a **spirometer trace** and know how these change from rest to exercise.

A spirometer trace

A spirometer is a machine that measures lung volumes.

As the individual breathes in and out a line is drawn by the spirometer, showing the depth and rate of breathing. This is called a spirometer trace.

Golden rule

Don't be put off if you see a spirometer trace. It will always show the lung volumes drawn on the diagram and described below.

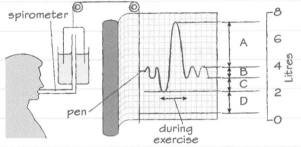

A Inspiratory reserve volume   C Expiratory reserve volume
B Tidal volume   D Residual volume

Key terms

Lung volume: refers to the capacity of the lungs (how much air they can hold). The greater the volume of the lungs, the more air they can hold.

Tidal volume: the amount of air inspired (inhaled) or expired (exhaled) in a normal breath.

Inspiratory reserve volume: the extra amount of air that can be forcibly breathed in, in addition to tidal volume.

Expiratory reserve volume: the additional amount of air that can be forcibly breathed out, in addition to tidal volume.

Residual volume: the amount of air that always remains in the lungs, even after the forced maximal exhalation.

Lung volumes on a spirometer trace

Changes to tidal volume during exercise

When the body is at rest, breathing is slower and shallower than when exercising. This is because the demand for energy is less.

During exercise, you need to increase airflow into and out of your lungs. This is because:

• you need to get more oxygen into your lungs, so it can diffuse into the bloodstream for additional energy production

• you need to breathe out the additional carbon dioxide produced during exercise.

To allow this to happen, tidal volume will increase.

Worked example

Michael is taking part in a training session where he works maximally for a short period then rests before working maximally again.

Figure 1

Analyse the spirometer trace in **Figure 1**.
Consider when:
(a) Michael is working maximally
Where the lines become much larger
(b) Michael is recovering
Immediately after the last highest point

Now try this

(a) Justify your answers to the Worked example above. **(4 marks)**
(b) Copy and complete the trace to show the likely change in lung volume when Michael works maximally again. **(1 mark)**

Aerobic and anaerobic exercise

Exercise can be either **aerobic** or **anaerobic**. You need to understand these terms and the equations and physical activities associated with them.

Aerobic or anaerobic?

The length and/or the intensity of the exercise will determine how the energy for the exercise is produced.

Aerobic exercise is exercise in the presence of enough oxygen.

- It uses oxygen for energy production when exercise is steady and not too fast.
- At such times the heart can supply all the oxygen that the working muscles need to produce energy aerobically.

Examples: Longer duration, low-intensity activities such as long-distance running or jogging up and down the pitch in a game of football.

Anaerobic exercise is exercise in the absence of enough oxygen.

- It **does not** use oxygen in energy production when exercise duration is short and at high intensity.
- At such times, the heart and lungs cannot supply blood and oxygen to muscles as fast as the respiring cells need them, so energy is produced anaerobically.

Examples: Short-duration, high-intensity activities such as javelin, shot put, and 400 m and 100 m sprinting

Anaerobic exercise includes short-duration, high-intensity activities such as javelin.

Summary of aerobic exercise

GLUCOSE + OXYGEN → ENERGY + CARBON DIOXIDE + WATER

- Glucose and oxygen combine to release energy aerobically.
- This process produces carbon dioxide and water in addition to releasing energy.

Carbon dioxide is a waste product. During exercise it is produced at a faster rate, so more carbon dioxide needs to be removed from the body when exercising.

Summary of anaerobic exercise

Carbohydrates are broken down without oxygen during anaerobic exercise to form glucose.

GLUCOSE → ENERGY + LACTIC ACID

- Without oxygen, lactic acid accumulates (builds up) in the blood and muscle tissue.
- This causes muscles to become tired and work less efficiently.
- This causes a drop in performance.

Lactic acid is a by-product of anaerobic energy production.

Worked example

This is a straightforward question. Say what you know about the production of carbon dioxide during exercise.

State why carbon dioxide levels increase during aerobic activities such as running a marathon. **(1 mark)**

They increase because CO_2 is produced at a faster rate during aerobic exercise than at rest.

Now try this

Using an example from a sport of your choice, identify when that sport will provide:
(a) aerobic exercise
(b) anaerobic exercise. **(2 marks)**

Excess post-exercise oxygen consumption (EPOC)

You need to be able to provide a definition of **EPOC**, show you understand why it happens and what this means to the performer.

Excess post-exercise oxygen consumption (EPOC)

EPOC is the additional amount of oxygen consumed **after anaerobic** exercise, during the recovery period, above what would usually be consumed at rest.

Sometimes EPOC is referred to as oxygen debt (though this is now an outdated term).

EPOC:

- refers to the amount of oxygen needed to recover after exercise

- enables lactic acid to be converted to glucose, carbon dioxide and water (using oxygen)

- explains why we continue to breathe deeply and quickly after vigorous exercise.

Anaerobic exercise
produces ⬇
lactic acid
removed/ ⬇
broken down
after exercise
by ⬇
taking in more O_2 than at rest
by ⬇
maintaining elevated breathing rate

Don't be put off by the terminology. The title is actually very helpful in explaining the meaning of the term.

Analysing EPOC

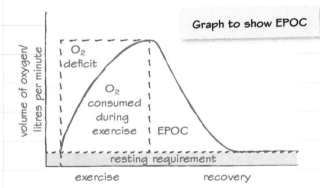

Graph to show EPOC

volume of oxygen/ litres per minute
O_2 deficit
O_2 consumed during exercise
EPOC
resting requirement
exercise   recovery

Things to note about the graph:

- It identifies the resting requirement for oxygen.
- The oxygen requirement during exercise is much higher than that required at rest.
- There is an oxygen deficit; this means not all the required oxygen can be provided.
- The demand for oxygen remains higher than the resting requirement, even after exercise.

Worked example

Although oxygen requirement drops after exercise, it is still higher than at rest.

Using the graph above, explain why oxygen requirement does not return immediately to resting levels after anaerobic exercise. **(4 marks)**

The graph shows an oxygen deficit during exercise. This is because the person was working anaerobically, so we can see that additional oxygen was consumed after exercise (EPOC) above resting requirement, in order to break down the lactic acid produced.

You will have experienced EPOC after a hard training session. It is when you breathe heavily after exercise to take in extra oxygen, to help you recover.

Make sure you reference the graph if directed to do so in a question.

Now try this

Explain when and why EPOC occurs. **(4 marks)**

Recovery from exercise

You need to be able to evaluate the use of the different methods of recovery. This means you need to be able to make a judgement about why these methods would or would not be used in recovery from different sporting activities. See page 64 for details on cooling down.

Massage

A qualified massage therapist rubs the muscles following vigorous exercise, to help prevent DOMS.

DOMS is **delayed onset muscle soreness**. DOMS does not occur immediately after exercise, but one or two days after a period of intense exercise.

The massage:
* reduces inflammation of tender area
* increases blood flow, so increasing oxygen delivery to the muscles and the removal of lactic acid.

Example: tennis players may use massage to help recovery after a long hard match

Ice baths

Getting into a bath of icy water for 5 to 10 minutes after lengthy or intense activity is thought to:
* aid the repair of micro-tears in muscle fibres
* reduce swelling of the injured area
* help prevent DOMS
* constrict the blood vessels to the muscles, reducing blood flow, so that when the performer gets out of the ice bath into warmer temperatures and the vessels dilate, oxygenated blood rushes to the muscles and helps remove lactic acid and other waste products.

Example: rugby players may have an ice bath after a gruelling rugby match

Manipulation of diet – carbohydrates

Food high in **carbohydrates** should be consumed soon after exercise, to replace glycogen stores used during activity.

In the two hours following strenuous activity, carbohydrates are converted to glycogen more quickly.

Example: Endurance performers, such as marathon runners, manipulate their diet in this way to replace energy stores.

Manipulation of diet – rehydration

Water or isotonic drinks should be consumed immediately after (as well as before and during) strenuous exercise to replace fluids lost during such exercise.

When we sweat during physical activity we lose water and salt. If these levels are not maintained we can become dehydrated, leading to dizziness and nausea.

Any performer who sweats must drink water after activity to rehydrate.

The questions require you to explain, so you need to say what happens and why.

Figure 1 shows an athlete using an ice bath. Explain why athletes use ice baths after vigorous exercise.   **(4 marks)**

Ice baths help reduce the risk of DOMS, by restricting blood flow to the muscles while in the ice, so once the athlete is out of it and warmer, there is increased blood flow to the muscles. This delivers additional oxygen to the muscles and reduces muscle tissue damage.

Figure 1

Make sure you reference both types of athletes in your answer.

Explain why a triathlete is more likely to manipulate his carbohydrate intake after exercise compared to a 100m runner.
   (4 marks)

25

Effects of exercise 1

Physical activity has several different effects on the body. You need to know what these are and why they happen.

The effects of exercise: key terms

Effects of exercise can be:

- **immediate** (the effects **during** exercise)
- **short-term** (the effects **24 to 36** hours **after** exercise)
- **long-term** (the effects **after months** or **years** of training).

 If a question refers to one of these terms, make sure you relate your answer to the correct time period.

Immediate effects of exercise

1 **Getting hot**: Heat is a by-product of energy production, so when you exercise you get hot. The more strenuous the exercise, the hotter you will get.

2 **Getting sweaty**: Sweat glands produce sweat to try to cool you down, and the sweat evaporating from the surface of your skin removes some body heat.

3 **Having red skin**: Blood vessels dilate to increase blood flow near to the surface of the skin, to help you lose heat this makes you look red. The heat is lost through radiation from the surface of the skin.

4 **Increased depth and frequency of breathing** allows gaseous exchange to occur more quickly:
- More oxygen can be moved into the blood from the lungs to supply the working muscles.
- More carbon dioxide can be removed from the blood into the lungs and breathed out.

5 **Increased heart rate** means gases can be transported more effectively to allow:
- increased oxygen delivery to the working muscles
- increased removal of carbon dioxide from the working muscles.

Short-term effects of exercise

1 **Tiredness/fatigue** as energy stores are used up during the activity

2 **Light headedness and/or nausea** due to dehydration and depleted energy stores

3 **Aching muscles** due to not cooling down properly after exercise

4 **Cramp** as a result of depletion of energy stores or dehydration and lack of electrolytes (such as salt and potassium) due to sweating during exercise

5 **DOMS** due to micro-tears in the muscles caused by the activity

Muscles may be sore the day after a hard training session, due to DOMS.

Now try this

One immediate effect of exercise is increased frequency of breathing.
Explain the advantage of this immediate effect of exercise to a games player.   **(3 marks)**

Effects of exercise 2

Regular training and exercise will benefit the body owing to the gradual training adaptations. These long-term effects of exercise may take months or years to achieve, and many of them link to components of fitness. Turn to page 59 to revise training zones.

What are the long-term effects?

Body shape may change, for example an increase in muscle mass or drop in excess fat

Improved stamina

Increase in the size of the heart (cardiac hypertrophy)

Lower resting heart rate (bradycardia)

Why are these effects beneficial?

Useful for activities requiring strength or power, or activities where excess fat is a disadvantage, for example long distance running

Able to last longer in an activity

Good for fitness, as the heart can contract more forcefully and eject more blood per beat to supply the required oxygen

Greater training zone: Together with an increased stroke volume, the heart needs to beat less often to eject the same amount of blood

Improvements in specific components of fitness

Long-term effects of months or years of exercise can also improve specific components of fitness, for example it can:

- **build muscle strength**, so improving the player's **ability** to overcome a resistance, so they could bring down an opponent more easily when tackling

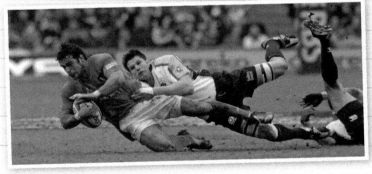

- **improve suppleness/ flexibility**, so improving the player's range of movement at a joint, so they can stretch further without causing injury

- **build cardiovascular endurance**, so improving the ability of the player's heart and lungs to supply oxygen to the working muscles, so the player can work for the whole duration of the game

- **improve speed**, so improving the player's rate of performing movements quickly, so the player can run more quickly to score

- **improve muscular endurance**, so improving the ability of the player's muscles to undergo repeated contractions and avoid **fatigue**, so keeping performance at a high standard throughout the game.

Turn to pages 33–40 to revise the components of fitness.

Worked example

Make sure you give a long-term effect on the heart.

Ria plans to sustain her involvement in exercise and physical activity. Identify one long-term effect of participation in exercise on Ria's heart. **(1 mark)**

Ria's heart will undergo hypertrophy.

Now try this

Describe one way in which the muscular system is affected by regular exercise and the long-term benefit of this on the performer. **(2 marks)**

Lever systems 1

Lever systems help you to move. They can increase the amount you can lift or increase the speed at which you can move something. You need to be able to sketch and label the three classes of lever correctly and give examples of their use in sport.

Levers and lever systems

A **lever** is a rigid bar that rotates around a fulcrum to apply a force to a load (resistance).

Within the body:

- the **lever** is a bone
- the **fulcrum** (or pivot) is a joint
- the **effort** (or force) is provided by muscles
- the weight of the body part or object being moved is the **load** (resistance).

There are also levers outside of the body, for example, a racket used to apply force to a ball.

There are three classes of lever system. Each class has the same components but they are arranged in a different order.

The same shape is always used to represent each component of a lever system.

The fulcrum is shown as a triangle. **F**

The effort is an arrow (pointing in the direction that the effort is applied). **E**

The load (resistance) is a square. **L**

The lever is a straight line. ──

The order of the components determines the class of lever.

First class lever system

L ──────── **E**
F

The fulcrum is between the load and the effort.

In this attacking header, the head coming down on the ball is the **load**, the **fulcrum** is the atlas and axis joint, and the muscles allowing the head to move in this way provide the **effort**.

Second class lever system

L ──── **E**
F

The load is between the effort and the fulcrum.

During calf raises (plantar flexion at the ankle), the ball of the foot is the **fulcrum**; the gastrocnemius provides the **effort** to lift the whole body weight, and the weights being held are the **load**.

First class lever – extending the arm at the elbow

Extending the arm at the elbow is another first class lever. This is because the triceps muscle attaches to the ulna at the elbow, to provide the effort. The fulcrum (the elbow) is in the centre of the lever system.

Worked example

What component of a lever system is represented by a triangle? **(1 mark)**

A Fulcrum ●   C Effort ☐
B Lever ☐   D Load ☐

You will need to learn these symbols so you can sketch the lever systems.

Figure 1

Now try this

(a) Using the symbols on **Figure 1** as a guide, identify the lever system being used by the rower.

(b) Give a reason for your choice. **(2 marks)**

Lever systems 2

In addition to the three classes of lever, you need to know the term **mechanical advantage** and how it relates to each of the lever systems.

Third class lever

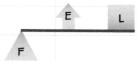

The effort is between the load and the fulcrum.

Third class levers are the most common lever systems in the human body.

An example of a third class lever is a biceps curl (flexion and extension at the elbow). The fulcrum is the elbow joint, the load is the weight being lifted, and the effort is provided by the biceps pulling the lever (the bone) to lift the weight.

Third class lever – biceps curl

Mechanical advantage

The design of each lever gives it its own benefits; these are due to the lever's **effort arm** and **resistance arm**.

- The effort arm is where the force is applied to the lever. It is shown by drawing an arrow between the **fulcrum** and the **effort**.

- The resistance arm moves the load. It is shown by drawing an arrow between the **fulcrum** and the load (resistance).

Identifying lever systems

Each lever system can be identified by the component in the middle. Remember the following rhyme:

One,	two,	three
	=	
'F'	'L'	'E'
(fulcrum)	(load)	(effort)

Then you can remember the component in the middle and therefore name the class of lever.

Class of lever

Mechanical advantage

First class lever
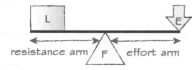
Will vary depending on the distance of the load/effort from the fulcrum

Second class lever
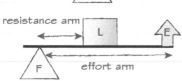
Able to lift heavier loads, owing to its long effort arm

Remember: mechanical advantage = effort arm ÷ weight (resistance) arm.

Third class lever
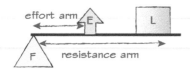
Provides speed and wide range of movement owing to long resistance arm

Worked example

Identify the lever system operating at the knee when kicking a ball. **(1 mark)**

Third class lever

You do not need to explain your answer, as the question just asks you to identify the lever system.

Now try this

Explain the mechanical advantage of the lever system at the ball of the foot in a sprint start. **(3 marks)**

Remember to justify your answer by linking back to the question about a sprint start.

Planes and axes of movement 1

We move in **planes** around **axes**. You need to be able to identify and describe the three different body planes and axes.

Planes of movement

A plane is an imaginary line that movement direction occurs in.

You need to know the names and direction of the three different planes.

- The **sagittal plane** divides the left and right side of the body, vertically.
- The **frontal plane** divides the front and the back of the body, vertically.
- The **transverse plane** divides the top and bottom of the body, horizontally.

Axes of movement

An axis is a line about which the body/body part can turn.

You need to know the names and direction of the three different axes.

- The **sagittal axis** goes from front to back.
- The **transverse axis** goes from side to side.
- The **longitudinal axis** goes from top to bottom.

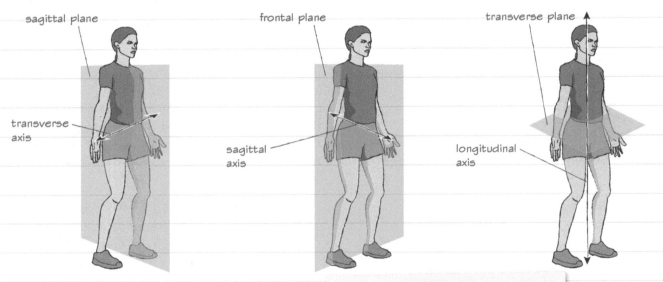

The three planes and axes of movement

Golden rule

- ✓ Movement in the **sagittal** plane can only be around the **transverse** axis, for example when performing a forward roll.
- ✓ Movement in the **frontal** plane can only be around the **sagittal** axis, for example when performing a cartwheel.
- ✓ Movement in the **transverse** plane can only be around the **longitudinal** axis, for example when performing a 360° twist (ice skating spin).

Worked example

Which is the correct description of the sagittal plane? **(1 mark)**

A Divides the body from left to right ⬤
B Divides the body from top to bottom ◯
C Divides the body from inside to out ◯
D Divides the body from back to front ◯

 Now try this

 Make sure you answer **both** parts of the question.

Describe the direction of the transverse axis and name the plane linked with this axis. **(2 marks)**

Planes and axes of movement 2

Only certain movements can happen in each plane and around each axis. You need to be able to link the different movement possibilities to each plane and each axis, giving examples from sport.

Sagittal plane and transverse axis

The **only** movements that can occur in the sagittal plane about the transverse axis are:

- **flexion**
- **extension**.

A somersault is performed in the sagittal plane about the transverse axis.

Frontal plane and sagittal axis

The **only** movements that can occur in the frontal plane about the sagittal axis are:

- **abduction**
- **adduction**.

A cartwheel is performed in the frontal plane about the sagittal axis.

Transverse plane and longitudinal axis

The **only** movements that can occur in the transverse plane about the longitudinal axis are:

- **rotation**
- **twisting**.

A full twist is performed in the transverse plane about the longitudinal axis.

Worked example

Identify the movement possible in the sagittal plane.   **(1 mark)**

A Abduction   ○   C Circumduction   ○

B Extension   ●   D Adduction   ○

Remember the rules: flexion and extension are the **only** movement possibilities in the sagittal plane, so the answer must be extension.

Summary table of movement for planes and axes

Sagittal plane	Frontal plane	Transverse plane
Divides the left and right side of the body, vertically	Divides the front and back of the body, vertically	Divides the top and bottom of the body, horizontally
Flexion and extension	Abduction and adduction	Rotation
Rotation around the transverse axis	Rotation around the sagittal axis	Rotation around the longitudinal axis
The transverse axis goes from side to side	The sagittal axis goes from front to back	The longitudinal axis goes from top to bottom
Used in a somersault or running action, for example	Used in a cartwheel, for example	Used by a discus thrower rotating in the circle, for example

Now try this

Think about the direction that the axis must be going in to allow rotation in this direction.

As part of their routine, a gymnast may perform a back somersault.
Name the plane the movement occurs in **and** the axis about which the movement occurs.   **(2 marks)**

Had a look ☐ Nearly there ☐ Nailed it! ☐

The relationship between health and fitness

You need to know the definitions of and the relationships between **health** and **fitness** and the role that training or exercise plays in this relationship.

Key terms

Health: a state of complete physical, mental and social **well-being**, and not merely the absence of disease or infirmity.

Ill health: a state of poor physical, mental and/or social well-being.

Fitness: the ability to meet/cope with the demands of the environment.

Golden rule

Remember: exercise **must** be regular to be effective.

regular exercise

increased fitness

increased performance

health benefits

Factors working together

Regular **exercise** plays an important role in increasing health, fitness and performance.

- If you take part in regular exercise, you can increase your fitness.
- If your fitness improves, your performance can improve too.

For example:

> If your cardiovascular fitness improves
>
> ↓
>
> you are less likely to suffer with fatigue
>
> ↓
>
> so you can maintain your level of performance for longer.

Factors not working together

> If you are not healthy enough to take part in regular exercise
>
> ↓
>
> your fitness will deteriorate
>
> ↓
>
> causing your performance levels to drop
>
> ↓
>
> and health benefits will not be gained.

Golden rule

Remember: sometimes people are unhealthy but are still able to train and therefore fitness can still be increased.

Worked example

Which of the following is a true statement about the relationship between exercise, health and fitness? **(1 mark)**

A You need to be healthy in order to be fit. ☐
B If you exercise regularly you can guarantee that you will improve health as well as fitness. ☐
C It is possible to be fit but not healthy. ●
D Whatever the intensity, exercise will improve health. ☐

First, discount the obvious.
D starts with 'whatever the intensity', which isn't true as it is possible to overtrain and cause health issues.
B is false – it makes it more likely, but doesn't guarantee it.
That leaves A or C. Option C is correct – you could be fit but have a temporary illness like a cold, and therefore not be healthy.

Now try this

Explain the relationship between health and exercise. **(3 marks)**

Agility

You need to be able to define the different components of fitness and be able to justify their importance across a range of activities. One of these components is **agility**.

Definition of agility

Agility is the **ability** to move and change direction quickly (at speed) while maintaining control.

> **Golden rule**
>
> Note the three components of agility:
>
> **1** The ability to **change direction**
>
> **2** The ability to do so **quickly**
>
> **3** The ability to do so with **control**

Describing agility

The best way to **describe** agility is: to change direction quickly with control.

It is needed in activities where you are going in one direction and then very quickly change to a different direction, perhaps to avoid an opponent.

You need to include both 'change direction quickly' **and** 'with control' to describe agility accurately.

Ask yourself: how does being able to change direction quickly impact on performance in the sports below?

Agility in sport

Agility is very important to all games players where there is direct interaction between teams, for example, in games such as rugby, netball and football.

Agility is needed to get free from or to dodge tackles, for example, when swerving around a player.

Agility is also important in racket sports, such as badminton, tennis and squash.

Badminton players need to change direction quickly with control, depending on where the shuttlecock has been played.

> **Golden rule**
>
> Always choose an example you are sure about and use words like 'dodge' and 'swerve' when talking about agility.

When is agility not important?

Agility is not normally important for activities where there is no interaction. Think of a 50 m swimming race in a 50 m pool. The swimmer has their own lane, so no one can interact with them. They only have to go one length in a straight line, so they do not need to change direction.

However, if the race is 100 m in a 50 m pool, then the swimmer will use agility to turn quickly to swim in the opposite direction.

Worked example

State how a basketball player will use agility in their sport. **(1 mark)**

The player will sidestep to change direction quickly with control, to avoid being tackled when dribbling down the court.

Notice how the response has been linked to the activity and uses all aspects of agility: 'change direction', 'quickly' and 'control'.

Now try this

Briefly explain how agility might be useful to a performer batting in cricket just after they have played a good shot. **(2 marks)**

Remember: What is it? Why is it important? What is the impact on the activity?

Balance and coordination

You need to know what **balance** and **coordination** are and why they are important, and to be able to give examples of how they are used in a variety of different activities.

Definition of balance

Balance is the maintenance of the centre of mass over the base of support. Balance can be **static** (stationary) or **dynamic** (moving). Balance is all about keeping steady to get the best result in performance.

Static balance

Static balance is when there is **no** movement and the performer needs to hold the position still.

Static balance is important to the gymnast so she does not fall or wobble and lose points for the quality of her movement.

Dynamic balance

Dynamic balance is balance while moving in an activity.

Dynamic balance is important to the hammer thrower so he maintains balance while turning and does not step out of the area, causing a foul throw.

Both types of balance are important to the performers.

Definition of coordination

Coordination is the ability to use different (two or more) parts of the body together, smoothly and efficiently.

Coordinated movement needs to be controlled so the end result is:

- efficient
- smooth
- effective.

All physical activities require good coordination to be successful.

Describing coordination

When describing coordination you **must**:

☑ mention that it involves **two** or more body parts

☑ mention that they are used **at the same time** or **together**.

For example, a tennis player will need to use their hand and eyes together to ensure successful contact is made between the ball and the racket in order to play an effective shot.

 Worked example

Briefly explain how a football player uses coordination to take a shot at goal.   **(2 marks)**

The player will use foot–eye coordination so that the foot accurately makes contact with the ball. This will enable them to execute the technique correctly, making good contact and increasing the accuracy of their shot at the goal.

When answering questions about coordination you need to be very clear about:
- which two body parts are coordinating
- why this is good
- what the impact will be on performance.

 Now try this

Describe the difference between how coordination is used by a golfer taking a putt and a swimmer during a 100 m butterfly race.   **(4 marks)**

Cardiovascular endurance

You need to know what **cardiovascular endurance (aerobic power)** is and why it is important, and be able to give examples of how it is used in a variety of different activities.

Definition of cardiovascular endurance

Cardiovascular endurance is the ability of the heart and lungs to supply oxygen to the working muscles.

Remember to include both parts of this definition – mention 'heart' and 'lungs' as well as 'oxygen' and 'working muscles', as these points are key!
Always write cardiovascular rather than the abbreviation CV, to show that you really do know the words.

Golden rule

Don't confuse the terms 'cardiovascular endurance' and 'cardiovascular system'. They are closely linked, as cardiovascular endurance relies on the cardiovascular system supplying oxygen, but they are not the same thing.

Good cardiovascular endurance can be a health benefit, for example reducing the chance of coronary heart disease (CHD).

When we need cardiovascular endurance

Cardiovascular endurance is required when activities:

* are mainly aerobic
* last a long time
* involve prolonged additional oxygen delivery.

It is used by performers who need to:

* maintain quality of performance over a long time, such as games players
* work the body for long periods of time without tiring, such as long-distance runners.

What, who, why and how?

When you are thinking about the components of fitness, you should ask yourself four questions:

☑ What is it?
☑ Who needs it?
☑ Why is it important?
☑ How does this affect performance?

Cardiovascular endurance can also be referred to as aerobic power or aerobic fitness.

Worked example

Through training an individual may improve aspects of fitness.
Which one of the following gives the best explanation of cardiovascular endurance? **(1 mark)**

A The ability to use the muscles of the body for long periods of time without fatigue.
B The ability to exercise the heart for long periods of time.
C The ability of the heart and lungs to supply oxygen to the working muscles.
D The ability of the heart and lungs to supply blood to the muscles.

○
○
●
○

 At first several answers look promising, but option A only mentions muscles, option B only mentions the heart, and although option D does state 'heart and lungs' it does not mention 'oxygen' or 'working muscles', making option C the only one that has all relevant parts of the definition of cardiovascular endurance.

Now try this

Jo and Jus both play rugby. Cardiovascular endurance is an important component of fitness for rugby players. Briefly explain why Jo and Jus need high levels of cardiovascular endurance to perform well in their sport.
(2 marks)

Flexibility

You need to know what **flexibility** is, who it is important to, and the advantages it brings to the performer if they have high levels of it.

Flexibility

Flexibility is defined as:

'the range of movements possible at a joint'

Flexibility is important in **all** activities.

> **Golden rule**
>
> Ask yourself:
> - ☑ What is it?
> - ☑ Who needs it?
> - ☑ Why is it important?
> - ☑ How does this affect performance?

Flexibility is important as it:

- increases the range of movements at the joint, allowing the performer to reach further
- helps prevent injury.

Some examples of flexibility are more obvious than others. You can see the wide range of movement at the hip and back of this gymnast.

The importance of flexibility to performers

You need to be able to give examples of how good flexibility benefits performance.

In the examples below, note the linking words 'so' and 'because', which are used to link a fact about flexibility to its application to the activity.

Good flexibility allows the netball player to stretch further so she can intercept the ball.

Good flexibility prevents injury to the footballer when overstretching because the joint can move further before damage occurs.

Worked example

Identify how the performer on the left in **Figure 1** is using flexibility in their activity. **(1 mark)**

The performer is using flexibility so they can reach further to get the ball.

> The question asks you to 'identify', so there is no need to give a justification for your answer.

Figure 1

Now try this

Sue and Jenny both play basketball. Flexibility is an important component of fitness needed when playing basketball. Briefly explain why Sue and Jenny need high levels of flexibility to perform well in their sport. **(2 marks)**

> If you are asked to 'explain', don't just give a definition. You need to **give a reason why** it is important, which could be through the use of an example.

Muscular endurance

You need to know what **muscular endurance** is and why it may (or may not) be needed when performing certain physical activities and sports.

Definition of muscular endurance

Muscular endurance is the ability of a muscle or muscle group to undergo repeated contractions, avoiding fatigue.

Golden rule

If you use a definition, make sure it is enough to answer the question. If you are asked to apply something or give an example, the definition on its own will not be enough.

Avoiding confusion

Muscular endurance is:

☑ different from cardiovascular endurance – make sure you mention muscles!

☑ different from muscular strength, which is to do with force. 'Endurance' means it has to last a long time without tiring.

When we need muscular endurance

Muscular endurance is required when activities:

- are mainly aerobic
- last a long time
- require repeated use of the same muscles.

It is used by performers who need:

- prolonged additional oxygen delivery to working muscles
- to repeat muscle contractions over a long period of time **without tiring.**

Cardiovascular endurance works with muscular endurance as the heart and lungs need to supply sufficient oxygen to the working muscles so that they can contract repeatedly for a long duration.

Worked example

Define the term 'muscular endurance'.   **(1 mark)**

The ability of a muscle or muscle group to undergo repeated contractions, avoiding fatigue.

Key words to include in your answer: 'muscles', 'repeated', 'without fatigue'.

EXAM ALERT!

It is a good idea to learn definitions for when a question states '**define**'. If a question asks you to describe or explain, you should use your own words.

Now try this

Make sure you refer to Ashley's training sessions in your answer.

Ashley has joined a rowing club and trains three times a week, rowing at least 3 km every session. He is improving his muscular endurance.

Explain the term muscular endurance, using an example of how Ashley would use muscular endurance in his training sessions.   **(3 marks)**

Power and speed

You need to know what the components of fitness, **power** and **speed**, are and why they are important in a range of physical activities and sports.

Power

Power is the product of strength and speed, or strength x speed.

Power can also be referred to as explosive strength or anaerobic power.

This gymnast has used power to get height, so he has time to perform the move well and score points for technique.

Golden rule

Power is all about using strength at speed. Therefore any examples you give of power must demonstrate high intensity **and** explosive movements.

Speed

Speed is the maximum rate at which an individual is able to perform a movement or cover a distance in a period of time, putting the body parts into action as quickly as possible.

It is calculated by distance ÷ time.

- Speed is vital in any race – a runner, cyclist or speed skater would all depend on speed.
- Speed can be vital for other movements too – a javelin thrower needs to be able to bring their arm through very fast to get the maximum distance with the javelin.

Speed is useful:

- where events are won by the quickest time
- to gain an advantage over opponents, for example, beating them to a loose ball in football.

Who and how?

- 100 m sprinter: to beat the opponents and get a faster time.
- Marathon runner: in a sprint finish.
- Long jumper in the run up: to jump further.
- Javelin thrower having a fast arm: to increase throwing distance.

Figure 1

Worked example

Figure 1 shows a table tennis player taking part in a match. Explain, using an example, why speed is important in a table tennis match. **(3 marks)**

The player uses speed to move their arm quickly. If their arm moves quickly they can put more pace on the ball, making the shot harder for their opponent to return, and so they are more likely to win the point.

Make sure you use the word 'quickly' rather than just 'moving the arm', as the arm could be moved slowly for a soft shot. Include a justification, as the question asks you to 'explain'.

Now try this

Power is important to many different activities.
Complete the table below about power and add a different example of your own. **(5 marks)**

Who	Power used to:	Impact
Sprinter	(i)	An explosive start
Basketball player	(ii)	Close to hoop to score
(iii)	(iv)	(v)

Reaction time

You need to know what **reaction time** is and why it is important. You also need to be able to give examples of how reaction time is used and its importance in a variety of activities.

Reaction time

Reaction time is how long it takes to respond to a stimulus.

For example, in the 100 m sprint, it is the time from the starting gun firing (the stimulus) to the sprinters starting to move out of the blocks (the moment when they first respond).

Fast reaction times are useful in events where quick decisions about movements are needed. They help performers:

- to get a good start
- to adapt quickly to rapid changes in play (normally game situations).

Golden rule

When considering reaction times, always ask:

- ✓ Who? (For example, 100 m sprinters)
- ✓ What is the stimulus they respond to? (For example, starting pistol)
- ✓ Why is it important? (For example, to get the best start)
- ✓ How does this impact on performance? (For example, the sprinters are more likely to finish more quickly.)

Identifying the stimulus

Think of different things that can be a stimulus in sporting activities:

- a ball
- a whistle
- an error
- a dangerous situation
- a starting pistol
- an opponent

You can anticipate that something is going to happen or it may just happen suddenly, but as soon as you detect the stimulus you need to decide on a **course of action**.

Although a good reaction time would be useful at certain points in all of these sports, it is most important here for the swimmer – so they can leave the blocks quickly to win the race.

 Worked example

Which of the following performers is most likely to benefit from a fast reaction time? **(1 mark)**

A Rugby player performing a drop kick ☐
B Badminton player playing a smash shot ☐
C Basketball player performing a lay-up ☐
D Swimmer leaving the starting blocks ●

Examples of needing quick reaction time

- A rugby player changing direction owing to a deflected ball.
- A badminton player deciding to play a different shot after their opponent has 'dummied their shot'.
- A goalkeeper diving to save a sudden shot at goal.
- A gymnast needing to make a sudden adjustment to an error.
- A rock climber losing their footing.

Think of the benefits to each performer.

In sprint activities, a fraction of a second can make the difference between winning and losing.

 Now try this

Figure 1

Using **Figure 1**, explain the importance of reaction time to a tennis player. **(3 marks)**

Remember to use the image to guide your answer.

Strength

You need to know what **strength** is and the difference between each type of strength. You also need to know why strength is important when performing certain physical activities and sports.

Strength

Strength is the ability to overcome a resistance.

Strength requires a force to be applied by a muscle or muscle group.

Strength can be:

1 maximal

2 static

3 dynamic

4 explosive.

Maximal strength

Definition: the maximum force that can be generated by a muscle or muscle group.

Example: Power lifters use maximal strength when attempting to lift the heaviest weight they can.

Static strength

Definition: when the muscles apply force but the muscle length stays the same. (Static means staying still.)

Example: Performers use static strength when applying a force to an immoveable object such as the floor; for example, a gymnast holding a plank position or opposing teams in rugby holding a scrum position.

Dynamic strength

Definition: when the muscles are applying force repeatedly. (Dynamic means moving.) Similar to muscular endurance and also known as strength endurance.

Example: A gymnastic uses dynamic strength when moving their body weight throughout the length of the routine on a pommel horse.

Explosive strength

Definition: another name for power, where force is applied at speed.

Example: A discus thrower uses explosive strength during their rotation and release of the discus.

A gymnast using dynamic strength during a pommel horse routine.

If a question asks you to give more than one example, make sure you use different examples for each performer.

Worked example

Complete the table below by giving an example of how strength would be used by each performer. **(3 marks)**

Performer	How strength is used in their activity
Sprinter	The sprinter would use explosive strength to apply a greater force against the ground or starting block, to decrease the time taken to run the race.
Rugby player	A rugby player would use strength to stop himself being barged off the ball; this would allow him to maintain possession.
Weightlifter	A weightlifter would use static strength to support a heavy weight above his head at the end of the lift for a short period of time.

Now try this

Figure 1

State how the gymnast is using static strength in **Figure 1**. **(1 mark)**

Fitness testing

You need to know the general reasons for carrying out fitness tests and the potential limitations of fitness testing.

Reasons for fitness testing

Before a **training** programme:
- 👍 To identify strengths and areas for improvement
- 👍 To identify training requirements
- 👍 To show a starting level of fitness
- 👍 To motivate
- 👍 To provide goals

During and **after** a training programme:
- 👍 To monitor improvement
- 👍 To provide variety to a training programme
- 👍 To compare results against norms of the group/national averages
- 👍 To identify whether training has been successful

Limitations of fitness testing

- 👎 Tests are often too general and are not sport-specific.
- 👎 The movement required in the test is not the same as in the actual activity.
- 👎 Tests do not have the competitive conditions required in sports.
- 👎 Some tests do not use direct measuring and are an estimate or are **submaximal**.
- 👎 Some tests need motivation, because they are exhausting to complete.
- 👎 Some tests have questionable **reliability**.
- 👎 Tests must be carried out using the correct procedures to increase **validity**.
- 👎 These limitations can lead to inaccurate results.

Key terms

Norms (normative data): data collected from a large sample of the population for use in fitness rating charts, used to compare own fitness test results with national averages.

Maximal: working at the highest intensity possible.

Submaximal: working below maximal intensity level.

Reliability: the consistency and repeatability of a test (does the test produce the same or similar scores each time?).

Validity: the extent to which a test measures what it sets out to measure.

Golden rule

Fitness tests can be used:
- ✓ at the start of an exercise programme
- ✓ during a programme, to monitor how the training is going
- ✓ at the end of the programme, to see if the training was effective.

Remember: fitness tests are **not** used to improve fitness, just to measure it.

Note the question states 'best' describes. Make sure you read all of the options before making your decision.

Worked example

Which one of these best describes the validity of a fitness test? **(1 mark)**
A A fitness test that gives repeatable results. ☐
B A fitness test that tests what it says it tests. ⬤
C A fitness test that makes the performer work maximally. ☐
D A fitness test that is sports-specific. ☐

Option A describes a reliable test; option C is incorrect, as not all fitness tests require maximal work; option D is incorrect, as although this might be useful it doesn't mean the test is measuring what it claims to be measuring. Option B is the correct option.

 Now try this

State **three** reasons why a coach may use fitness testing with his team. **(3 marks)**

Agility and speed tests

You need to be able to select when the fitness tests below would be relevant, based on the specific components of fitness required by a performer, and evaluate their relevance for different sporting activities. You also need to know how these tests are carried out, the facilities and equipment required, and how both tests are measured.

Illinois agility test

Test of **agility**

Used by: performers who need to change direction quickly, such as:
- basketball players
- rugby players.

Facilities/equipment:
- Flat running area
- Cones, measuring tape, stopwatch

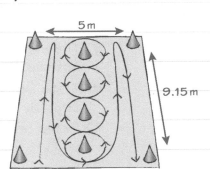
5 m
9.15 m

Test procedure:

1 Set up the course (as shown in the picture).

2 Lie face down on the floor by the first cone.

3 On 'Go', run round the course as fast as possible.

4 Record the time taken.

5 Compare your result to a rating chart.

Both the Illinois agility test and the 30 m sprint test are measured in seconds (sec).

30 m sprint test

Test of **speed**.

Used by: performers who need to run fast for a short time, such as:
- 100 m sprinters
- rugby players.

Facilities/equipment:
- Flat running area (over 30 m)
- Measuring tape, stopwatch

In many sports, performers need to be able to sprint, partially recover, and then sprint again.

Test procedure:

1 Measure and mark out 30 m in a straight line.

2 Place one cone at the start and one at the end.

3 On 'Go', run as fast as you can.

4 Record the time taken.

5 Compare your result to a rating chart.

Worked example

Name the fitness test being described below. Start from a stationary position and when told to 'go', run as fast as possible in a straight line. **(1 mark)**

30 m sprint test

Most tests will start from a stationary position, so this part of the description doesn't really help. However, the description then says 'run as fast as possible'. That implies speed, so it could be the Illinois agility test or the 30 m sprint Test. The final part of the description says 'in a straight line' so must be referring to the 30 m sprint test, as the Illinois agility test requires changes in direction.

Now try this

Imran plays for the school football team. At the start of the season the team undergoes a series of fitness tests. In the table below:
- tick the most relevant fitness test for a football player (not goalkeeper)
- explain why this fitness test is most relevant to Imran. **(3 marks)**

Fitness tests	Tick (✓)	Explanation: why this fitness test is the most relevant to Imran
Illinois agility test		
Handgrip dynamometer test		
Sit and reach test		

Coordination and reaction time tests

You need to be able to select the appropriate fitness tests for coordination and reaction time and be able to evaluate whether these tests are relevant to performers in different sporting activities.

You need to know the procedures, facilities and equipment required for each test and how it is measured. All fitness test results are compared to rating charts, to determine the performer's level of fitness.

Wall toss test

Test of (hand–eye) **coordination**

Used by: performers who need to use two or more body parts together smoothly and effectively, such as:

- badminton players
- cricket fielders

Facilities/equipment:

- Wall
- Tennis ball
- Stopwatch

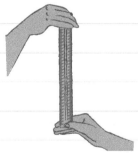

Test procedure:

1. Stand 2 m away from a wall.

2. Throw a tennis ball underarm against the wall.

3. Throw with the right hand; then catch with the left hand; then alternate hands.

Measured by: number of throws and catches achieved in 30 seconds (sec).

Ruler drop test

Test of **reaction time**

Used by: performers who need to respond to a stimulus quickly, such as:

- 100 m sprinters
- games players

Facilities/equipment:

- A ruler
- Assistant

Test procedure:

1. An assistant holds a ruler.

2. Stand with your hand open around the ruler, with the 0 cm mark between thumb and forefinger.

3. The assistant drops the ruler (without warning).

4. Catch ruler as quickly as possible, between thumb and forefinger.

Measured by: how far the ruler dropped in cm.

Worked example

Identify the correct item of equipment to test coordination.

(1 mark)

A Mat ○
B Ruler ○
C Cone ○
D Tennis ball ●

Option B, a ruler, can be discounted immediately. While a mat might provide somewhere to stand and a cone could be used to mark the 2 m distance, they are not the essential items needed to complete the test. Therefore, option D is the only possible correct answer.

Now try this

Name the component of fitness tested by the ruler drop test and describe the procedure for completing this test.

(3 marks)

43

Cardiovascular endurance and balance tests

You need to be able to select the appropriate fitness tests for cardiovascular endurance and balance. There are several different tests for cardiovascular endurance, but the test and procedure that you need to know is the multi stage fitness test (MSFT).

Multi stage fitness test

Test of **cardiovascular endurance** (aerobic power)

Used by: performers who need to supply oxygen to the working muscles for a long time, such as:

- games players
- long-distance runners/swimmers.

Facilities/equipment:

- Flat running area (over 20 m)
- Recording of the bleep sounds
- Measuring tape
- Cones

20 m

Test procedure:

1. Measure out 20 metres.
2. Place cones to mark the distance.
3. Start the audio recording.
4. Run from one cone to the other, reaching the 2nd cone before the next bleep. The time between bleeps gets progressively faster, meaning you have to get faster. Keep going until you cannot reach the cone before the next bleep.

Measured by: the level reached and the number of shuttles completed at that level.

Stork balance test

Test of **balance**

Used by: performers who need to maintain their centre of mass over their base of support, such as:

- gymnasts
- games players.

Facilities/equipment:

- Stopwatch

Test procedure:

1. Place your hands on your hips.
2. Place your non-balancing foot against the other knee.
3. Raise your heel from the ground so you are balancing on your toes (timing starts when you lift your heel).

Measured by: how long you can hold the balance in seconds (sec).

Worked example

Which one of these states an item of equipment needed to carry out the stork balance test? **(1 mark)**

A A bench   ⬭   ☐ C A mat   ⬭
B A stopwatch   ⬤   ☐ D A whistle   ⬭

The only item of equipment needed for the stork balance test is a stopwatch; therefore option B is the correct answer.

Now try this

Identify **two** pieces of equipment required for the multi stage fitness test and describe how each piece is used. **(4 marks)**

Look for the key words in the question. For this question, make sure you talk about **two** pieces of equipment.

Strength and flexibility tests

You need to be able to select the appropriate fitness tests for flexibility and strength. You also need to evaluate when two different types of strength test would be most relevant, based on performers in different sporting activities.

Handgrip dynamometer test

Test of **strength** (hand and forearm)

Used by: performers who need to apply a force against a resistance, such as:

- rock climbers (using hands to lift body weight).

Facilities/equipment:

- Handgrip dynamometer

Test procedure:

1 Adjust the grip to fit your hand.

2 Keep your arm beside and at a right angle to the body.

3 Squeeze the handle as hard as you can.

Measured by: reading scale and comparing to ratings chart (recorded in kg).

One rep max test (1RM)

Test of **maximal strength**

Used by: performers who need short bursts of maximum force, such as:

- power lifters
- rugby players.

Facilities/equipment: Free weights

Test procedure:

1 Warm up.

2 Lift the maximum weight you can in one attempt.

3 Compare your result to a rating chart.

Measured by: amount of weight lifted (kg).

Sit and reach test

Test of **flexibility** (lower back and hamstrings)

Used by: performers who need a wide range of movement, such as:

- gymnasts
- hurdlers.

Facilities/equipment:
- Sit and reach box

Test procedure:

1 Sit with your legs straight and the soles of your feet flat against the box.

2 With palms face down, one hand on top of the other on the box top, stretch and reach as far as possible.

3 Record the distance reached.

4 Compare your result to a rating chart.

Measured by: distance reached in cm.

Worked example

Discuss the value of the handgrip dynamometer test for measuring strength relevant to sprinting. **(3 marks)**

The handgrip dynamometer test is a test of strength so has some relevance, but it is a measure of grip strength, not the strength required by sprinters. Therefore it would be better to find a test that related to leg strength for the sprinters.

If a question starts with the word 'Discuss', this normally means that you need to think of good points and bad points. This answer identifies a good point (tests strength) ✓, a bad point (leg strength more relevant to sprinters) ✓ and concludes (look for a test for leg strength) ✓.

Now try this

Liam is 14 years old. He has returned to gymnastics after injury. He completed the sit and reach test and scored 23 cm. Explain how Liam's coach would use the information from this fitness test. **(3 marks)**

Rating	Age (years)				
	12	13	14	15	16
Good	29	30	33	34	36
Average	26	26	28	30	30
Below average	20	21	23	24	25

Power and muscular endurance tests

You need to know the difference between the following two fitness tests. Power tests are short, explosive tests whereas muscular endurance tests use repeated muscle contractions.

Vertical jump test

Test of **power**/explosive strength (anaerobic power)

Used by: performers who need to perform strength activities quickly, such as:

- sprinters
- rugby players.

Facilities/equipment:

- Wall
- Ruler/measuring tape
- Chalk

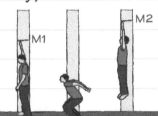

Test procedure:

1. Stand side-on to a wall, feet flat on the floor.
2. Mark the highest point that the tips of your fingers can reach with the arm closest to the wall.
3. Holding a piece of chalk in the hand closest to the wall, jump as high as you can (upwards).
4. Mark the wall at the top of the jump.
5. Measure the difference between the first and second chalk marks.
6. Compare your result to a rating chart.

Measured by: distance reached in cm.

Sit-up bleep test

Test of **muscular endurance**

Used by: performers who need to use repeated muscle contractions for a long time and maintain quality of performance, such as:

- tennis players
- football players.

Facilities/equipment:

- Recording of the bleep sounds
- Mat

Test procedure:

1. Lie on a mat, knees bent, feet flat on the floor.
2. Place your arms across your chest, with hands on opposite shoulders.
3. Start the audio recording.
4. Sit up until your back is at 90° then return to the start position.
5. Sit up in time with the audio track, one sit-up every 3 seconds (20 per minute) until you cannot complete any more.
6. Compare your result to a rating chart.

Measured by: number of sit-ups completed.

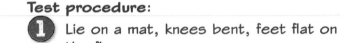

Worked example

As the question asks for an explanation you need to justify your answer.

Explain whether you would use the sit-up bleep test or vertical jump test with a high jump performer. **(4 marks)**

The sit-up bleep test is a test of muscular endurance whereas the vertical jump test is a test of power. A high jumper does not need muscular endurance as their event is explosive, but they do need power to clear the bar, therefore they should use the vertical jump test.

Now try this

State why the sit-up bleep test would be relevant to test the fitness of a rower. **(2 marks)**

Fitness testing: data collection

You need to know how test scores are measured and compared to national averages. To do this you need to be able to collect and interpret data from fitness tests and analyse and evaluate the results.

Collecting data

When collecting results from a series of fitness tests you will need to produce a **data collection sheet**. This should include:

- the date
- the name of the test
- your result
- the outcome based on your comparison to the relevant rating chart.

This will help you see if your training programme has been successful.

Key terms

Raw data: the score from your fitness test.

Interpret: using the data tables to provide a rating of your fitness.

Analyse: breaking down the information to determine where your strengths/ weaknesses are, based on the test results.

Evaluate: making a judgement, based on looking at the data, about the impact of training.

Qualitative or quantitative?

When collecting pieces of data for fitness tests they are usually **quantitative**, meaning:

- the measurements can be quantified as numbers, such as time in seconds or distance in centimetres
- they are facts.

Data can also be **qualitative**, meaning:

- the measurements are based on the quality rather than the quantity, such as a number out of 10 for a routine
- they are opinions rather than facts.

Quantitative fitness test scores

These are measured/recorded in:

- seconds, how fast
- levels, how far through recording
- centimetres, how far
- numbers, how many.

Golden rule

Quantitative data collected during fitness testing can be compared to national averages to obtain a level of fitness.

Data for tests for this exam are quantitative, but you need to know the difference between the terms.

Worked example

The table shows normative data for the multi stage fitness test.
Evan is 19 years old and his younger sister Nell is 14. They both achieved 44 in the multi stage fitness test.
Use the table to interpret and evaluate their results. **(3 marks)**

	Age	Excellent	Good	Average	Below Average
Males	15–19	>60	48–59	39–47	30–38
Females	15–19	<54	43–53	35–42	28–34

Evan's result of 44 shows that his rating is average. Nell's result places her as good. Although they both achieved the same score, the chart shows that Nell's rating is higher than Evan's, so he may wish to work more on this aspect in his training.

Find the score on the chart to determine the rating and then evaluate the information.

Now try this

State why it is important to analyse and evaluate fitness test results. **(2 marks)**

Principles of training 1

To improve your fitness you need to train. When planning a training programme you need to use the **principles of training**. You need to understand these and be able to apply them to bring about improvements in fitness, as well as apply them to sporting examples.

Principles of training

For training to be successful it is important that you do not train too little or too much. It is also important that the training is right for each person, and will help them to improve. Therefore you need to apply the principles of training.

Golden rule

Do not confuse **principles** of training with **types** of training.

- ✓ Principles are the things you need to consider when planning your training programme.
- ✓ Types are the ways you complete your training.

S-P-O-R-T

The principles you need to take into account when planning training are:

- S = Specificity
- P
  O = Progressive Overload
- R = Reversibility
- T = Tedium

Golden rule

You can use the acronym **SPORT** to help you remember the names of the principles of training. Some of these principles should be applied and some should be avoided; however, you need to consider them all.

Specificity

Description: Specificity means matching training to the particular requirements of an activity.

Explanation: You must make sure that your training is appropriate for your sport. This is so that you are training the right muscles and body systems, rather than other areas of fitness that will have little impact on your performance.

Application: For specificity, a rower could plan their training around using a rowing machine.

Training

Activity

Using a treadmill instead of a rowing machine might train some of the same things but would not be the best match.

Which of the following statements does **not** conform to the principle of specificity? **(1 mark)**

A A 100 m runner practising their sprint starts. ○

B A games player taking part in a fartlek training session. ○

C A tennis player practising their first serves. ○

D A 50 m freestyle swimmer working on their speed at the track. ● ⬅ The swimmer should be training in the pool rather than on the track.

Figure 1

Three items of fitness training equipment are shown in **Figure 1**.

Explain which of the items of equipment shown is most likely to be used by a sprint cyclist. **(3 marks)**

Principles of training 2

There are three key principles of training on this page – **progressive overload**, reversibility and tedium. One you need to use in your training and the other two you need to plan to avoid.

Progressive overload

Progressive overload must show an increase in training over time and it must be gradual so that no injuries occur.

Description:

Progressive overload means gradually increasing the amount of work in training so that fitness gains occur, but without the potential for injury.

Explanation:

You need to gradually increase intensity in training so that the body continues to increase fitness.

Application:

- Week 1 = do 5 sit ups
- Week 2 = do 10 sit ups

Don't confuse the word 'overload' with 'overuse'. You should overload but not overuse, which is forcing yourself beyond your capabilities.

Reversibility

This means that any improvement or change that takes place as a consequence of training will be reversed when you stop training.

Just as fitness can be increased through training, the benefits will be lost if training stops owing to injury or a holiday.

Training needs to be regular so that adaptations gained through training are not lost. Remember if you stop training, reversibility will occur!

Tedium

This is the boredom that can occur when you train the same way every time.

Gaining improvements in fitness and performance is a gradual process and takes a long time, so variety in training is needed in order to keep interested and motivated to carry on and not give up.

For example, you could vary the activities in a circuit or weight training session, or vary the route of a running course.

Briefly explain the principle of progressive overload, and state how it can improve fitness. **(2 marks)**

Progressive overload means gradually increasing the work you do. For example, if you lift heavier weights, you will get stronger, therefore fitter, because the body adapts to the new workload.

There needs to be a definition and an example, a link between the principle and why fitness increases. It would not be enough to just say you get stronger.

Elad wants to improve his cardiovascular endurance by developing an exercise programme based on continuous training.
Explain how Elad could use progressive overload to improve his cardiovascular endurance. **(3 marks)**

Principles of training 3

You need to be able to apply the key principles of overload using the components of the **FITT principle**: frequency, intensity, time and type.

FITT: Frequency

This is about **how often** you train. It should be gradually increased, for example:

Once a fortnight to start with → Once a week → Twice a week

Training more often can lead to improved performance.

FITT: Intensity

This is about **how hard** you train. It should be gradually increased, for example:

* 1 set of 5 repetitions of a 5 kg weight.
* 2 sets of 5 repetitions of a 5 kg weight.
* 2 sets of 5 repetitions of a 10 kg weight.

Training harder can lead to improved performance.

FITT: Time

This is about **how long** you train. It should be gradually increased, for example:

Session 1 = 20 minutes → Session 2 = 25 minutes → Session 3 = 30 minutes

Training for longer can lead to improved performance.

FITT: Type

This relates to specificity. The closer the match between training and activity, the better the improvement in performance.

For example, a marathon runner would use continuous training rather than weight training, although muscles would benefit from weight training. A continuous running training programme would be more closely related to the activity and be more likely to train the correct muscles and body systems.

Worked example

As part of her training programme, Eve was asked how she applied the FITT principle.
Describe how Eve could apply **one** of the components of the FITT principle. **(2 marks)**

Eve could increase the frequency of her training. She may have started training once a week and increased it to twice a week in the second week of her programme.

Overlap with other principles

The FITT components should be taken into account when applying progressive overload, but remember the principle of overtraining and its impact.

◄ If asked to describe one principle, you can choose any, so choose the one that you understand the best.

Now try this

The FITT principle of training is made up of four parts. Which of the following statements covers all four parts? **(1 mark)**

A How hard and often you work, making sure you do not do too much, while avoiding boredom ☐

B How long, hard and often you work, while maintaining safety ☐

C How hard and often you work, making sure that your training fits the requirements of the activity, and that you do not do too much ☐

D How long, hard and often you work, making sure that your training fits the requirements of the activity ☐

Circuit training

Types of training are used to improve fitness and performance levels. You need to know several different types of training and be able to select and evaluate the appropriate type for various fitness needs.

Circuit training is very adaptable and involves a chain of different activities that can be selected to suit individual or activity requirements.

Training can be used to develop all of the components of fitness depending on the nature of the stations included, e.g.
- sit-ups for muscular endurance
- shuttle runs for speed
- dodging through cones for agility
- balancing ball for balance.

There are a number of stations (usually between 6 and 12).

The stations are organised in a circuit, so that you can progress from one station to the next.

Characteristics and benefits of circuit training

The stations can be fitness- or skill-based.

The variety of stations allows recovery of muscle groups (so anaerobic work is possible).

The circuit can be organised so that it is continuous, usually done with 30–60-second breaks while leaving one station and getting in position at the next – **interval training**.

Aerobic circuit training will have the health benefits associated with this type of activity, for example, weight loss (if overweight) through burning additional calories.

The intensity can be measured by:
- the **time** at each station
- the **number of repetitions** at each station
- the **number of circuits** completed.

Depending on the intensity of the activity, circuit training can be aerobic (low intensity) or anaerobic (high intensity).

Golden rule

When using **any** training type you must take account of:
- ☑ the training purpose(s)
- ☑ training thresholds
- ☑ training targets
- ☑ training zones
- ☑ rest/recovery.

When planning a circuit, you specifically need to consider:
- ☑ the space available
- ☑ the number of stations for your needs
- ☑ time working to time resting (the work:rest ratio).

Worked example

George is 15 years old. He has designed a circuit to help improve his performance in basketball and badminton.

Four of the circuit stations are listed below:

Station 1 – running in and out of cones

Station 2 – lay-up shots using a basketball

Station 3 – bowling at a target

Station 4 – badminton serves.

Explain why **one** of these stations is not appropriate for George's circuit. **(2 marks)**

Station 3, bowling at a target, does not relate to either of his sports.

Now try this

State **three** characteristics of circuit training.   **(3 marks)**

 Remember: **do not** use fitness tests as circuit stations.

Continuous training

You need to know what **continuous training** is and when it would be an appropriate type of training to use.

Aerobic or anaerobic

You need to know which types of training should be used to develop fitness for aerobic activities, and which for anaerobic activities.

- Interval training is used more for anaerobic activities.
- Continuous training is aerobic and is therefore used more for aerobic, endurance-based activities.

Aerobic activities are **submaximal**. This means you do not work flat out and so can continue to work for long periods of time.

Continuous training characteristics

In continuous training, each training session:

- should involve sustained exercise at a constant rate (steady state)
- must not involve any breaks or rests during the session
- should be for 20 minutes or longer (so there is an aerobic demand).

Continuous training should be used for activities that reflect these characteristics, such as long-distance running, swimming, rowing and cycling.

For example, a runner could run at a steady pace around a 400 m track for 30 minutes (without stopping).

Continuous training: benefits

Components of fitness that would improve with continuous training include:

- cardiovascular endurance
- muscular endurance.

Regular continuous training can reduce the chance of coronary heart disease and related illnesses.

It can also reduce the risk of osteoporosis if the training is weight bearing.

Continuous training is non-stop exercise at a steady pace without rest, involving aerobic demand for a minimum of 20 minutes.

Golden rule

All types of training, if done on a regular basis over a period of time, will bring about fitness adaptations, such as:

 lower resting heart rate   decreased recovery time.

 Worked example

What type of activity would an athlete probably be involved in if they only used continuous training to improve their fitness?   **(1 mark)**

They are likely to be involved in an endurance event, for example, marathon running.

Remember that 'athlete' is a term that can be used to mean any sports performer, not just those participating in 'athletics'.

 Now try this

Briefly explain why a long-distance runner would use continuous training as their main training method.

(2 marks)

Fartlek training

Fartlek training is a form of continuous training. Its key characteristics are variations in speed, terrain covered and work-to-rest ratios.

Key benefits

Jogging on the road

Sprinting on the road

Grassy hill

Changes of pace allow for recovery so the performer can work maximally.

Fartlek training improves cardiovascular endurance and muscular endurance and reduces the chance of coronary heart disease.

Fartlek training is continuous, but the changes in pace within the sessions mean that performers work both aerobically (jogging) and anaerobically (sprinting, running uphill) within the exercise session.

Activities associated with fartlek training

(Netball)   (Hockey)   (Rugby)   (Basketball)

This is due to the similarity between the training types and the game situation where there is sprinting and recovery, for example, making a fast break in hockey and then jogging back into position.

Worked example

Some training activities can be **adapted** to suit different performance activities. How might a cross-country runner and a footballer adapt fartlek training to suit their own activity?

(2 marks)

A cross-country runner would focus on changing terrains, for example, running on grass and through mud.

A footballer would focus on variation in pace to match game requirements.

EXAM ALERT!

Make sure you read the questions carefully – you need to say how the training session is adapted, rather than just describing the training type.

Now try this

Think about what a games player does during the game.

If you are a games player, outline why should you involve jogging and sprinting in a fartlek session? **(2 marks)**

53

Interval training

You need to know what **interval training** is and when it would be an appropriate method of training to use.

Characteristics

This type of training has periods of intense activity, with breaks within the session to allow recovery.

A typical session is usually made up of:

- sets of high-intensity work (e.g. sprint)
- followed by rest or low-intensity work (active rest)
- followed by high-intensity work (e.g. sprint)
- followed by rest or low-intensity work (active rest).

Aerobic and anaerobic

Aerobic: 'with oxygen' (low-intensity, longer duration activities).

Anaerobic: 'without oxygen' (short-lived, explosive activities).

Benefits

- Aerobic interval training will have the health benefits associated with this type of activity, for example, weight loss (if overweight) due to burning calories.
- It is a very flexible training method that can be used to improve health and fitness in a range of ways.
- Although normally associated with powerful and explosive activities, it can be adapted to help improve cardiovascular endurance by altering the lengths of the rest periods.

If you are asked to name a type of training to improve cardiovascular endurance, only use interval training if you can **clearly** justify your answer by explaining how it can be adapted.

Forms of interval training

These include:

- training on a track
- circuit training
- weight training.

Although interval training can be designed for both aerobic and anaerobic activity, it is usually associated with shorter anaerobic events such as sprinting, and is a major form of training for sprint swimmers.

Interval training methods can be designed so that most components of fitness can be improved through an interval training programme. Strength could be improved if breaks are programmed in to a weight training session, for example:

- 10 reps arms, rest arms
- 10 reps legs, rest legs
- 10 reps arms, rest arms.

Worked example

Explain how you could tell by looking at a performer's interval training session plan if they were an endurance or power athlete. **(2 marks)**

The plan would include fewer rest intervals for an endurance athlete than for a power athlete, and less intense workload during periods of work for an endurance athlete compared to a power athlete.

Make sure you make it clear which type of performer you are talking about.

Now try this

Interval training is a method of training that can be used by a variety of performers.

Describe **three** characteristics of interval training. **(3 marks)**

'Characteristics' means things that are specific to that method of training.

Static stretching

There are several different methods of stretching that can be used for different purposes. The type of stretching you need to know as a specific type of training is **static stretching**.

Characteristics of static stretching

- You stretch as far as you can.
- The stretch is then held (**isometric**) for up to 30 seconds.

Key term

Isometric: a muscle contraction where the length of the muscle does not alter so the contraction remains constant.

Remember: correct technique must be used when completing any stretching, to avoid injury due to overstretching.

Benefits of static stretching

👍 Develops and increases flexibility

👍 Used to train for activities where an increase in range of movement at a joint is needed

Most activities that benefit from static stretching require good flexibility, such as:

- a hurdler reaching their leading leg over the hurdle while lifting their trailing leg to avoid knocking the hurdle down
- a football player stretching to intercept a ball
- a gymnast doing the splits.

How to use static stretching

You can work on your own, creating your own force to stretch the muscle.

You can use apparatus, for example a wall, thereby applying a force to an object that applies a force back, aiding the stretch.

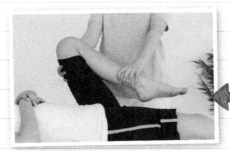

You can work with a partner, where a partner gently applies a force, helping to stretch the muscle further than you could on your own.

Now try this

Static stretching can be carried out with the help of a partner.
State why the use of a partner can be beneficial. **(1 mark)**

Weight training

You need to know how **weight training** can be carried out to develop different components of fitness.

Characteristics of weight training

Key characteristics:

- It is a form of **interval training** using weights.
- It involves 'reps and sets': the weights are lifted a number of times (reps), followed by a break before starting another set
- The weight provides a resistance or load for the muscles to work against.

Golden rule

When referring to this method of training, always make sure to use the terms **weight training** or **resistance training** and not weights or weightlifting.

Using weight training

Weight training can be completed by using machines or free weights.

The muscles you wish to train can be targeted by doing specific exercises, for example, biceps curls work on the biceps.

Benefits

Weight training can be used to develop fitness for many activities, the most obvious being those requiring **power** and **strength**, such as:

- weightlifting
- rugby
- shot put.

It can also be used for activities requiring **muscular endurance**, for example, tennis.

The components of fitness developed through weight training depend on the design of your training session.

For example:

- To develop **power** and **strength**, use high weight × low number of reps.
- To develop **muscular endurance**, use low weight × high number of reps.

Remember: when completing weight training it is important to use safe practice, including using correct lifting technique and spotters.

Worked example

Elaine has taken up discus and wants to know what training type to use to help improve her performance. Explain which training type she should use. **(2 marks)**

Elaine should use weight training as this will help her increase her strength so she can throw the discus further.

Make sure you answer both parts of the question. If you can justify your choice, you know you must have made a good decision.

Now try this

Endurance and power athletes will often use weight training as part of their training programme. Describe how weight training can be used to develop muscular strength or muscular endurance. **(2 marks)**

Plyometric training

You need to be able to decide when plyometric training would be an appropriate type of training to use.

Characteristics of plyometric training

- Jumping/bounding (often over obstacles)
- High intensity
- Short duration
- Breaks between sets
- Speed not endurance
- Maximal

Benefits of plyometric training

- Used to develop **power** by quickly lengthening and then quickly shortening muscles.
- Used to train for activities where there are fast, explosive movements, such as:
  - volleyball
  - basketball
  - hurdles.

Use of plyometric exercises

There are different types of plyometrics for different activities. The type of plyometrics you use will depend on:

- what you want to train for
- the resources available
- your level of fitness.

Plyometrics uses forceful bounding motions to stretch the muscles. An eccentric muscle contraction (where the muscle lengthens) is immediately followed by a larger concentric contraction (where the muscle then shortens).

Plyometrics can be completed by jumping onto boxes, jumping high and fast. This could be used when training for basketball, where the performer needs to jump high when taking a shot.

Worked example

Describe **two** ways that the intensity of plyometric training could be increased to provide progressive overload to a training session. **(2 marks)**

The training session can be adjusted so it gradually gets harder, for example, by gradually increasing the height of the box and also increasing the number of boxes.

> Make sure you include **two** answers. If you don't know the answer, think about the activity: what could you change to make it harder?

Now try this

Explain why plyometric training would be a suitable method of training for a volleyball player. **(3 marks)**

> Think of the activity (volleyball): think of the component of fitness that plyometric training will improve, and how a volleyball player uses this component of fitness in their sport.

Training types: pros and cons

You need to know the advantages and disadvantages of the different types of training. Think about things you like and don't like when doing each type.

Continuous training
- 👍 No equipment or facilities needed
- 👍 Can be done on your own or with others
- 👍 Health benefits (e.g. reduced chance of coronary heart disease)
- 👎 Can be boring, so motivation can be lost
- 👎 Doesn't change pace, so not so good for games players
- 👎 Can cause impact injuries

Fartlek training
- 👍 No equipment or facilities needed
- 👍 Can be done on your own or with others
- 👍 Change of pace/terrain can add interest
- 👎 Safe route not always easy to find
- 👎 Higher intensity parts can be avoided

Interval training
- 👍 No equipment needed
- 👍 Can be adapted for anaerobic or aerobic activity
- 👎 Can be repetitive and therefore boring
- 👎 Need to plan and keep track of sets

Static stretching
- 👍 Increases flexibility
- 👍 Anyone can do it safely
- 👎 Not as effective as some other stretching methods
- 👎 Takes a long time to go through all muscle groups

Weight/resistance training
- 👍 Easily adapted for muscular endurance or strength
- 👍 Can target specific areas of the body
- 👎 Equipment can be expensive
- 👎 Need to complete technique correctly to avoid injury
- 👎 Using free weights requires help from a spotter

Plyometric training
- 👍 Can be completed with no equipment
- 👎 Can cause injury owing to its high intensity if not carried out correctly

Circuit training
- 👍 Variety of stations generates interest
- 👍 Does not have to involve equipment
- 👍 Can be used to work on skill and fitness
- 👍 Can be aerobic or anaerobic by changing the time at stations/rest
- 👍 Easily adapted for each person
- 👎 If equipment is required, it can be costly
- 👎 Can take time to set up and put away
- 👎 Limited time at stations to work on skills
- 👎 Difficult to work on all skills

Does the method match the event?

Worked example

State a disadvantage of fartlek training for a sprinter. **(2 marks)**

Although fartlek includes sprints, a sprinter would not need to work on their cardiovascular endurance and when fartlek training would therefore not be focusing on their anaerobic system.

This is an 'explain' question, so refer to the impact on the performer.

Now try this

One disadvantage of continuous training is that it can get boring. Explain why this is a disadvantage. **(3 marks)**

Training intensities

When planning a training programme you need to set the relevant training thresholds.

Working in your training zone

To maximise the chance of fitness adaptations taking place, you should train within your target zone.

- The **training threshold** is defined as: the boundaries of the target zone.
- Your **target zone** is the range between the two training thresholds.

There will be an upper and a lower limit that you should be training between (training threshold).

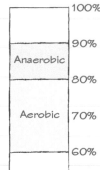

If your activity has lots of high intensity work, you should aim to work nearer the upper threshold of your target zone. Your anaerobic training zone is:

- 80 to 90% of your maximum heart rate (MHR).

If your activity is mainly low intensity or you wish to use fat as an energy source, you should aim to work nearer the lower threshold of your target zone. Your aerobic training zone is:

- 60 to 80% of your MHR.

Calculating training zones

- To calculate your **maximum heart rate (MHR)**, subtract your age from 220.
- To work out your **aerobic training zone** you calculate 60% and 80% of your MHR.
- To work out your **anaerobic training zone** you calculate 80% and 90% of your MHR.

For example: Bobbie is 16 years old.

$$220 - 16 = 204 \text{ (MHR)}$$
$$80 \times 204 \div 100 = 163 \text{ (80\%)}$$
$$60 \times 204 \div 100 = 122 \text{ (60\%)}$$

You can round figures up and down, so Bobbie's aerobic training zone is between 160 and 120 beats per minute (bpm).

Calculating one repetition maximum (one rep max or 1RM)

As part of weight training you might work out your 1RM, which is the maximum weight you can lift in one repetition. You can use this information to help you work out your training intensities, depending on whether you want to train to improve strength and power or muscular endurance.

- For strength/power training: high weight/ low reps above 70% of one rep max, approximately three sets of 4–8 reps.
- For muscular endurance: low weight/ high reps below 70% of one rep max, approximately three sets of 12–15 reps.

Circuit training intensities

Although some training methods require you to complete calculations to work out the correct intensity, other methods can be fairly simple. For example, in circuit training you can alter:

- the time spent at each station
- the amount of rest in between each station
- the content of the circuit.

Worked example

If the correct training zone for an endurance athlete is 120 to 160 bpm, how old is the athlete? **(1 mark)**

A 15 ☐ B 20 ● C 25 ☐ D 40 ☐

Use the target heart rate calculation to answer this question.

Now try this

State which of the lines on the graph (A, B, C or D) would indicate that Sulliman (aged 16) was working within his aerobic target zone while training? **(1 mark)**

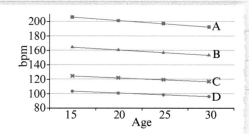

Injury prevention

When training, you also need to take into consideration how to prevent injury occurring. Some injury prevention factors apply to all activities and some will depend on the activity. You need to know when each should be considered.

Complete a warm up

A warm up should be completed to:

- increase the temperature in the muscles, tendons and ligaments
- increase elasticity
- help prevent a pull or a strain.
  For more on warming up, go to page 63.

Avoid overstretching

Stretches should be completed carefully without overstretching or bouncing, as this can result in muscle strain.

Avoid overtraining

If you train too hard, adaptations will not take place. For example, when weight training ensure you use the appropriate weight; if it is too heavy you may strain a muscle and not be able to improve.

Take adequate rest

Training programmes should include rest days. Make sure you have enough rest in between sessions to allow for recovery.

> Recovery is the time required to repair the damage to the body caused by training or competition.

Use taping and/or bracing

When necessary, taping or bracing, using items such as support bandages, should be used to provide additional support to joints, muscles or tendons. For example, this could include:

- taping the ankle to avoid a twisted ankle
- ankle bracing to reduce risk of ankle injury.

Remain hydrated

Maintain an appropriate level of hydration by drinking water. If you don't maintain your hydration levels you can become dehydrated, leading to dizziness and nausea.
For more on hydration, turn to page 109.

Wear appropriate clothing and footwear

This may include, for example:

- non-slip training shoes, to avoid twisting an ankle by slipping during a training session
- gum shields, to help protect teeth in impact activities such as rugby
- shin pads, to reduce the impact if hit by the stick in hockey.

> Remember: the type and intensity of your training should match the training purpose, to avoid causing injury.

Use correct technique

When completing any activity, using correct technique will:

- ensure better results
- help avoid injury, such as using the correct technique when lifting weights to avoid muscle strain.

Worked example

Which of the following statements gives the **most** important reason for wearing the correct clothing when taking part in physical activity? **(1 mark)**

A It gives you the opportunity to look good ⬭

B It gives you a psychological advantage over the opposition ⬭

C It reduces the chance of injury ⬤

D It is in the rules of physical activity ⬭

> Always watch for the word 'most'. Other statements may be true but are not the **most** important.

Now try this

State, using examples, **two** ways performers can help avoid injury in a game, in their preparation before the activity takes place. **(4 marks)**

High altitude training

In addition to the usual types of training, you need to know about the specific technique of **high altitude training** used as a form of aerobic training. Anywhere 2000 m above sea level or higher is considered to be high altitude. Turn to pages 51–57 for more on the different types of training.

Oxygen and high altitude

The percentages of the gases that make up the air are the same at sea level and at **altitude**, but there are fewer air molecules at altitude.

This means there is less oxygen available for us to take into our body. So, there is less oxygen to transfer from the lungs into the blood stream, and we can't carry as much oxygen to the working muscles. In other words, the body's oxygen-carrying capacity is reduced at high altitude.

Over time, the body compensates for this by making more red blood cells to carry oxygen.

Aerobic training at altitude

When an athlete first tries training at altitude their performance will be worse, as their oxygen-carrying capacity is reduced.

However, after several weeks of training at high altitude, their body will adapt by:

- increasing red blood cells
- increasing **haemoglobin**.

When they return to sea level (where there is more oxygen), they will have an advantage over competitors who have not completed high altitude training, because their body's oxygen-carrying capacity will have increased.

Benefits of high altitude training

👍 Increased red blood cell production

👍 Increased oxygen carrying capacity

👍 A greater amount of oxygen being transported to the working muscles once athletes return to sea level

These benefits are particularly helpful to endurance athletes who rely on aerobic energy production, for example triathletes or marathon runners.

Limitations of high altitude training

👎 Adaptations take time

👎 Expensive to live away from home

👎 Timing of training for competitions needs careful planning

👎 **Altitude sickness** (nausea caused by training at altitude)

👎 Limited/no effect on anaerobic activities, such as sprinting

👎 Can make it harder to train at the high intensities needed for anaerobic activities

Some athletes train low and sleep high, so they can train more effectively but benefit from the adaptations of living at high altitude.

Anywhere 2000 m above sea level or above is considered to be high altitude.

Worked example

(a) Which of these performers would train at high altitude?
100 m sprinter   10 000 m runner

(b) Justify your answer to (a).   **(4 marks)**

(a) The 10 000 m runner

(b) The 10 000 m runner works aerobically, so is reliant on oxygen throughout their race. This means they would benefit from the additional oxygen that could be carried by the body as a result of altitude training. The 100 m sprinter works anaerobically, so does not rely on oxygen in their event, so would not benefit from altitude training.

Don't forget to justify why you didn't select the 100 m sprinter, as well as justifying why you chose the 10 000 m runner.

Now try this

Explain **two** limitations of altitude training for a performer.   **(4 marks)**

61

Seasonal training

In order to peak at the perfect time for an event or competition, athletes need to carefully plan their training. To do this they divide their training into several seasons. You need to know the benefits of each **season** and be able to apply them to different sporting activities.

Pre-season (preparation phase)

This is the period leading up to competition.

Training includes:

- developing techniques specific to the sport
- general fitness training, such as continuous, fartlek or interval training sessions to increase aerobic fitness
- weight training to build up strength and muscular endurance.

Benefits

👍 Fitness and skill lost during post-season can be regained.

👍 Skills and techniques can be improved.

This means that matches at the start of the season can be more successful.

Competition season (peak)

This is the playing season.

Training includes:

- taking part in matches every week
- maintenance of fitness related to the activity
- limited training activity, as it may cause fatigue, which would decrease performance
- concentration on skills/set plays to improve team performance.

Benefits

👍 Fitness levels and quality of performance can be maintained throughout the season.

Post-season (transition phase)

This is the period of rest, active recovery and light aerobic work after the competition season.

Training includes:

- rest to recover from the competition season, where no training takes place
- light aerobic exercise, to maintain a level of general fitness.

Benefits

👍 Athletes are fully rested, ready for pre-season.

👍 Not too much fitness is lost.

Application of seasonal training to different activities

Seasons will vary depending on the activity.

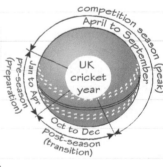

A possible cricket training year

A possible football training year

Other activities such as athletics and boxing will need planning in the same way, but will be around specific competitions.

Worked example

Explain why a sports performer would split their year into three training seasons. **(3 marks)**

This is so they are as fit as they can be and injury-free for the playing season. By resting after the competitive season (in the post-season) their bodies can recover, but this means fitness will be lost. This is therefore regained in the pre-season, so by the time of the playing season performers can focus on maintaining fitness and skill work.

Reference each of the training seasons, as they have been mentioned in the question.

Now try this

Identify the **three** training seasons. **(3 marks)**

Warm up

You need to know and be able to justify appropriate phases (parts) of a warm up for different sporting activities.

Warm up

You must know:

- the three phases of a warm up
- the order in which they occur
- examples of activities at each stage
- the significance of each stage.

Part 1 Pulse raiser

This gradually raises the heart rate and speeds up oxygen delivery, for example, jogging up and down the pitch.

Part 2 Stretching

Stretching the muscles and soft tissues you are about to use increases their elasticity and range of movement, for example, performing a hamstrings stretch.

Part 3 Skill-based practices/familiarisation

These should relate to the main session and allow more intense practices of skills through the whole range of movement, such as dribbling if you are about to play basketball.

Golden rule

A good warm up should take a minimum of 10 minutes and probably much longer, as it gradually increases the intensity at which the muscles are required to work (the effort) up to full pace.

Benefits of warming up

The benefits of a good warm up are extensive.

👍 It physically and mentally prepares you for exercise.

👍 It increases oxygen delivery to the working muscles.

👍 It increases the temperature of muscles, tendons and ligaments, reducing the chance of injury.

👍 It increases flexibility (range of movement), which will help performance.

Practices

The practices you do should mimic those you are about to use in the main session, in order to:

✓ help prepare muscles
✓ focus your mind
✓ rehearse the skills you are about to use.

Practise the skills you will use in the game as part of your warm up.

Worked example

State three phases of a warm up. **(3 marks)**

1 Pulse raiser   2 Stretching
3 More intense exercise/drill related to the main session

EXAM ALERT!

Students sometimes get confused by the term 'phases'. Make sure you give the three different phases, rather than examples of them.

Now try this

Three of the following statements relate to warm ups and their purpose. Which statement does not? **(1 mark)**

A The pulse raiser section of the warm up increases the amount of oxygen transported around the body ☐

B The warm up decreases the amount of lactic acid present and therefore reduces the likelihood of muscle soreness after the activity has finished ☐

C The warm up gets the performer mentally ready for the activity, as well as physically ready ☐

D The warm up increases the temperature of the body, resulting in it being better prepared for activity ☐

Cool down

You need to know and be able to justify appropriate phases (parts) of a cool down for different sporting activities.

Cool down

The purpose of a cool down is to return the body to its resting levels gradually, so there are no problems due to stopping exercise suddenly.

Golden rule

A cool down should **always** be completed after physical activity and sport.

Structure of a cool down

There are two stages of a cool down:

1 Light exercise to maintain an elevated breathing and heart rate, with a gradual reduction in intensity; for example, slow jogging to walking

2 Stretching of the muscles you have used in the main activity

A cool down is not designed to prevent injury – you should not get injured at this stage, as you have finished the main session and will be reducing the intensity of the work.

Benefits of cooling down

There are many benefits from a cool down, as it allows the body to recover and:

👍 prevents delayed onset of muscle soreness (DOMS)

👍 aids the removal of lactic acid, which can build up in the muscles

👍 aids the removal of carbon dioxide and other waste products

👍 helps bring the heart rate and breathing rate **slowly** back down to their resting rates

👍 helps avoid dizziness due to blood pooling in the lower limbs, which can happen if you suddenly stop exercising

👍 improves flexibility.

Stretching after an activity, while the muscles are warm, helps to improve flexibility.

For more on delayed onset of muscle soreness (DOMS), see page 25.

Worked example

Which of the following statements is a benefit of a cool down? **(1 mark)**

A It increases lactic acid production ☐

B It reduces the risk of muscle stiffness after exercise ●

C It <u>further</u> increases blood flow to the muscles after exercise ☐

D It reduces the chance of injury <u>during</u> the activity ☐

Option A isn't a benefit and is clearly incorrect; however, C and D could be thought correct if you only read the question quickly. Be careful to read all the words in each statement – the words underlined in C and D should show you these are incorrect answers.

EXAM ALERT!

Remember: you can cross through incorrect answers on the question paper as you work through the multiple choice questions.

Now try this

Choose words from the box below to complete the following statements about the cool down phase of an exercise session. **(6 marks)**

This takes place .... exercise. It is made up of .... phases. To begin with, the performer might carry out some light .... followed by .... Effective cool downs can reduce muscle .... and increase muscle ....

tension, after, strength, two, sprinting, during, four, skills, stretching, jogging, soreness, flexibility

Paper 1 – Extended answer question 1

There will be two extended answer questions at the end of each of your exam papers. One will be a 6-mark question and the other a 9-mark question. To gain all available marks for question 1 you will need to:

☑ demonstrate your knowledge and understanding of the topics related to the question

☑ apply the topics to relevant situations

☑ analyse and evaluate, making judgements about the things you have written.

For more detail on answering extended answer questions, turn to pages 115–116 in the Exam skills section.

Worked example

Evaluate the extent to which a warm up is necessary for a hockey goalkeeper. **(6 marks)**

The goalkeeper will complete a warm up before the match. They will complete a pulse raiser, such as jogging to the 23 metre line and back. This will raise the heart rate and get more oxygen to the working muscles so that energy is produced aerobically for the goalkeeper when they are constantly moving and getting into position to be ready to save any shot at goal.

The second phase of the warm up involves completing stretching exercises, stretching all the muscles the goalie is likely to use, for example, the hamstrings and quadriceps. Stretching will help increase the elasticity of the muscles, preventing a strain if the goalie overstretches when reaching out to prevent the ball going in the goal.

The final phase of the warm up is completing short drills, for example, saving shots at goal from various points around the 'D'. These help skills practice and mental focus, helping the keeper be alert and focused to save shots at goal in the match.

You could argue that a warm up is not important to a goalkeeper as they do not move as much as other players, and if they warm up they may just cool down again if not involved in play. However, it is still important, as once warm they would be ready for a sudden break at the start of the match, reducing risk of injury if they need to move at full stretch. They will also be ready psychologically, confident in their ability to block the shot. Without a warm up they would not be physically or mentally ready to play at their best.

When answering this question you will be assessed on your ability to **link ideas together** to show your understanding of different topics when applied to sport and physical activity.

Evaluate
An evaluation requires you to review information and bring it together to make a judgement based on the information you have presented.

For each point you make you should **give information about the topic**. Here you can see there is general information about a warm up and the purpose of the three phases. This knowledge has then been applied by linking specific examples to a hockey goalkeeper.

Use paragraphs to separate your points clearly.

Finally the response should make **judgements**. In this example these are made at the end of the response and are based on the points made previously. The **impact** on goalkeeper performance is considered as part of the evaluation.

Now try this

Explain the importance of redistribution of blood flow during a football match. **(6 marks)**

Paper 1 – Extended answer question 2

There will be two extended answer questions at the end of each of your exam papers. One will be a 6-mark question and the other a 9-mark question. To gain all available marks for question 2 you will need to:

- ✓ demonstrate your knowledge and understanding of the topics related to the question
- ✓ apply the topics to relevant situations
- ✓ evaluate what you have written to justify your answer.

For more detail on answering extended answer questions, turn to the Exam skills section on pages 112–117.

Worked example

Evaluate the selection of the handgrip dynamometer test and the multi stage fitness test to test the fitness of a netball performer before planning her training programme. **(9 marks)**

Plan – talk about both tests, apply both tests to netball, evaluate if they are the right tests for this performer.

Fitness testing is useful before starting a training programme as it can identify strengths and weaknesses that could then be addressed in training.

The handgrip dynamometer test can be used to measure strength and the multi stage fitness test can measure cardiovascular endurance.

Both of these components of fitness are relevant to a netball player. They need strong arms to ensure passes have enough force to get to their intended destination, and they need cardiovascular endurance so that they can keep playing for the whole match without tiring, meaning their performance would be better than someone with lower levels of cardiovascular endurance.

If the test results show that the levels of these two components need improving, the training programme can be designed to help. However, both tests have disadvantages. The handgrip dynamometer test only measures strength in the lower arm and hand, and if leg strength needs to be improved this would not be identified by this test. The multi stage fitness test is a maximal test. This means that the players have to be motivated to complete it – they must work their hardest in the test for it to be a true reflection of how hard they can work on the netball court. If they give up too soon the coach won't really know how well they could perform in a game of netball.

Look carefully at the question – the key word is **evaluate**, so you need to review the information you present. Fitness tests and netball are also mentioned, so you need to focus your response on these areas.

It is always a good idea to complete a brief plan to help focus your thoughts.

Start by demonstrating knowledge and understanding of the topics.

Then make specific links by applying your knowledge to relevant question context.

Finally, draw the information together to make judgements. Think of any negatives as well as the positives of the tests.

Now try this

When participating in physical activity there is always a risk of injury.
Evaluate the need for injury prevention methods in **two** contrasting physical activities, such as badminton and boxing. **(9 marks)**

Classification of skills 1

Many different skills are used to take part in sport. You need to be able to define the two terms – **skill** and **ability**, and be able to choose and justify the appropriate **skill classification** with sporting examples.

The difference between skill and ability

Skill is a **learned** action or behaviour with the intention of bringing about expected results, with maximum certainty and minimum outlay of time and energy.

Ability is an **inherited**, stable trait that determine an individual's potential to learn or acquire a skill.

Classification of skills

Some skills can be classified easily, as they are at one end or the other of a **continuum**.

A continuum is a line that goes between two extremes. Continua means more than one continuum.

However, many skills fall between the two ends of a continuum.

You need to classify skills on the following four continua:

open	closed
basic	complex
self-paced	externally paced
gross	fine

By thinking about the characteristics of each skill, you can position it at the right point along the continuum.

Open skills

Open skills are those that are affected by the surrounding environment.

Extreme **open** skills (at the far open end of the open–closed continuum) need to be constantly adapted by the performer to meet the requirements of the activity as situations change around them. Examples include:

- a pass in hockey
- dribbling in football
- a rugby tackle.

To account for the opposition or positioning of team members, open skills need adapting as they are executed.

With open skills, conditions are unstable and unlikely to be the same each time the skill is performed.

Closed skills

Closed skills are not affected by the surrounding environment or the performers within it.

Extreme **closed** skills (at the far closed end of the open–closed continuum) do not need to be adapted, because situations around the performer are stable. Examples include:

- a penalty kick in football
- a gymnastics vault
- a tennis serve.

Closed skills can be pre-planned. Opponents do not directly interact during the execution of the skill, reducing any sudden changes. The conditions are likely to be the same each time the skill is performed.

Worked example

Sports are made up of a variety of skills. Place the three skills from football on the continuum.
(i) Goalkeeper saving a penalty   **(ii)** Forward taking a penalty   **(iii)** Midfielder dribbling the ball   **(3 marks)**

open ●━━━━━━━━━━━━●━━━━━━━━━━━━━━━━━━━● closed

| midfielder dribbling the ball | goalkeeper saving a penalty | forward taking a penalty |

Now try this

When asked to 'define' there is no need to describe or explain – just say what it is.

Define the term 'open skill'.   **(1 mark)**

Classification of skills 2

You should be able to take any skill and place it at a point along any of the four continua.

Basic skills

Basic skills are those that:

- are simple
- require little thought
- do not need much information to be processed
- require little decision making.

Examples of skills at the extreme **basic** end of the continuum are:

- running
- cycling
- swimming
- a chest pass.

Complex skills

Complex skills are those that:

- are difficult
- require thought and concentration
- require a lot of information to be processed
- require a lot of decision making.

Examples of skills at the extreme **complex** end of the continuum are:

- trying to dribble past defenders
- rock climbing
- passing the baton in a relay race
- a lay up in basketball.

Self-paced skills

- The skill is started when the **performer decides** to start it.
- The performer controls the speed, rate or pace of the skill.

Examples of skills at the extreme **self-paced** end of the continuum are:

- serving in tennis
- bowling in cricket.

Externally paced skills

- The skill is started because of an **external factor**.
- External factors, such as an opponent, control the speed, rate or pace of the skill.

Examples of skills at the extreme **externally paced** end of the continuum are:

- receiving a serve in table tennis
- marking an opponent in basketball.

Gross skills

- Gross skills use big, strong, powerful movements.
- They involve the use of large muscle groups to perform.

Examples of skills at the extreme **gross** end of the continuum are:

- a tackle in rugby
- power lifting
- powerfully striking a football.

Fine skills

- Fine skills use small and precise movement, showing high levels of accuracy and coordination.
- They involve the use of a small group of muscles.

Examples of skills at the extreme **fine** end of the continuum are:

- a drop shot in badminton
- a short putt in golf.

Now try this

Think about how much harder it is to complete an overhead kick than a free kick in football – the performer has a lot more to think about when executing the skill.

Classify the following two football skills on a basic–complex continuum.
(a) Overhead kick
(b) Free kick
(2 marks)

Types of goal

You need to be able to define both **performance goals** and **outcome goals** and give examples of when each might be used.

Performance goals

Performance goals focus on your own **personal performance**. You can compare yourself against what you have already done or suggest what you aim to achieve. For example:

- I will use the correct grip every time I play a backhand drive in my next tennis match.

- Last match I completed three accurate long passes in netball; this match I will aim to complete five.

- I will increase weight lifted on the leg press from 15 kg to 20 kg for 10 reps.

👍 Performance goals are considered more appropriate than outcome goals as there is no comparison with other performers.

👍 As the focus is on improving personal performance, once the goals are achieved, the standard of performance will increase leading to more successful outcomes.

👍 Performance goals are therefore more motivating than outcome goals and can be achieved on your own, as they do not rely on others.

Outcome goals

Outcome goals focus on the **end result**, such as winning; they are literally the desired outcome of the game.

Performance and outcome goals can be combined; however, it is considered that setting outcome goals should be avoided, especially for beginners for whom winning may be an unrealistic goal.

For example, if an outcome goal was to win 4:2 and the actual result was a 1:6 defeat, this could result in performers becoming demotivated at not achieving their goal.

👍 Outcome goals can be used by more advanced players to motivate them to achieve the desired result.

👎 Some performers become so focused on the end result they do not focus on their actual performance, such as the good technique required for a successful result.

👎 As an individual you do not always have control over an outcome, as the end result also relies on input from others. Even if you play really well, the team may still lose, meaning the goal is not achieved.

Worked example

Explain why a coach would prefer his team had performance goals rather than outcome goals.
(3 marks)

The focus with these types of goals is on personal improvement rather than team outcomes, therefore they tend to be more motivating, leading to improvement.

Note the command word for this question. You must set out the reasons why the coach prefers performance goals.

Note how the answer first states what a performance goal is. This then makes it possible to state the reasons why this type of goal is preferable.

Now try this

Explain **one** reason why outcome goals may not be motivating. **(2 marks)**

Goal setting 1

You need to know the value of goal setting to improve and/or optimise performance in sport and physical activity. Remember that it is also important to **review** targets you have completed, so that you can see whether they were successful and use the results to set new targets.

Values of goal setting

Some of the values of setting goals are:

👍 increased motivation

👍 increased focus

👍 increased standard

👍 reduced anxiety

👍 improved monitoring of progress

👍 improved planning of training sessions (due to focus).

All these values can lead to improved performance.

SMART targets

In order for the goals you set to be successful, you need to use **SMART targets**. You need to apply all of them.

SMART stands for:

S = Specific

M = Measurable

A = Accepted

R = Realistic

T = Time bound

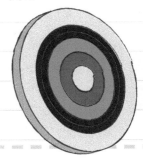

Specific (S)MART

Description:

Goals must be specific to the demands of the sport, such as the muscles or movements used.

Explanation:

A vague idea (for example, 'I must get better') is not **specific** or clear enough to provide the focus you need to bring about improved performance.

Application:

A specific and therefore clear target is:

To reduce the percentage of unforced errors in my passing from the centre third in netball.

> **Golden rule**
> Just saying 'to improve in netball' is too vague.

Measurable S(M)ART

Description:

In order to know if your goal has been met successfully, it must be something that can be measured.

Explanation:

The best way to measure something is to have units of measurement, for example, time, distances, numbers. Then you can measure whether the target has been achieved.

Application:

When giving examples of a measurable target make sure it has a number in it, for example:

To run 10 km **3 seconds** faster than my previous best.

> **Golden rule**
> Just saying 'to run a 10 km race faster' is too vague.

Worked example

Target setting should apply the SMART principle. State what the letter S in SMART represents and why it is important when setting targets. **(2 marks)**

The letter S stands for Specific – it is important to make sure that your target is clear so you know what you are aiming for.

Now try this

State why targets should be measurable. **(1 mark)**

Make sure you answer both parts of the question.

Goal setting 2

SMART targets must also be: Accepted, Realistic and Time bound. You will sometimes see alternative words for the SMART acronym, but these are the ones you need to know for this exam.

Accepted S M (A) R T

Description:

This is a target that is accepted by you and any others involved, such as your coach.

Explanation:

It means you must accept the target as something that you actually want to do. By committing to your target you will be more determined to achieve it. For your target to be something you can accept, you must believe you can achieve it.

Application:

I currently run 100m in 13 seconds. My goal is to run 100m in 12 seconds. My coach and I both accept we will work to achieve this.

Realistic S M A (R) T

Description:

A realistic goal is one that is possible, given all the factors involved.

Explanation:

Your goal might be achievable but are the other factors in place to make it realistic? For example, do you have access to training facilities, and do you have the time required?

Application:

I currently throw the javelin 30m. I am going to start an additional training session each week and my goal is to throw 35m by the end of this season.

Time bound S M A R (T)

Description:

Goals must be assigned a time frame for completion.

Explanation:

You need to have a cut-off point by which you should have achieved your goal, so that you can see whether your training is having the effect you want.

Application:

My goal is to run 200m in 45 seconds by 4 July this year.

Goals can be given a broad timeline, which may be:

• short term • medium term • long term.

You may have several short-term goals which are leading towards a long-term goal.

For example:

My **SMART** goal is: I currently average a goal a match in hockey. With additional practice I aim to average 2 goals per match by 30 December.

Worked example

Targets for sports performers should be realistic and time bound. Complete the table below by describing:
a) one consequence of setting unrealistic goals   b) one advantage of setting goals that are time bound. **(2 marks)**

a) Consequence of setting unrealistic goals	Performer would get demotivated and therefore stop training, causing a drop in performance rather than an improvement.
b) Advantage of setting goals that are time bound	Performer has a clear date by which to achieve their goal, so maintains motivation to complete it and beat the deadline.

Now try this

The SMART principle can help you set effective targets. The S of SMART stands for Specific. What does the letter R of SMART stand for?
(1 mark)

Information processing

You need to know the four stages of **information processing** and be able to explain them using skills from sporting examples.

What is information processing?

Information processing is where you make decisions based on gathering information (stimuli) from your senses, such as what you see and hear. You prioritise the most important stimuli to make a suitable decision.

1 **Input:** the information received from the display (your senses) via selective attention

2 **Decision making:** the selection of an appropriate response using the information 'input' and that stored in (long-term) memory

3 **Output:** information you send to your muscles to carry out the response

4 **Feedback:** a review of your response; this can be from yourself (intrinsic) and/or others (extrinsic)

Basic information processing model

Key terms

Long-term memory: This is information that has been rehearsed and stored for future reference. The more you practice, the more the technique is committed to long-term memory and the better it can be recalled.

Short-term memory: This only lasts a few seconds. This is the working memory you use while actually completing a skill, such as paying attention to your opponent's position as you catch a ball.

Selective attention: This is focusing on the important information (stimuli). When completing skills there can be a lot of information (stimuli) around you. You have very little time to select the relevant information (such as the speed of a ball) and ignore the irrelevant (such as a noise nearby).

Information processing in sport

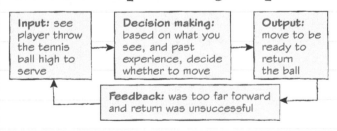

Feedback loops back to input, so the next time the player receives a serve from the same opponent the model might read:

Input – see the server throw high

Decision making – decide to move back

Output – move back, ready to return the ball

Feedback – return successful owing to perfect position to return that service

Worked example

Note the command word. You must set out the reasons why selective attention is important.

Explain, using an example, why selective attention is important in team games. **(4 marks)**

Selective attention is the ability to filter information so you can discount what's not relevant. Then you can focus on the important stimuli so you can make a quicker decision. For example, if a badminton player focuses on their opponent and not the crowd, they will be better able to process information about where the opponent's shot is going and how to respond.

Now try this

You will need to link four points together to gain maximum marks.

Describe **one** difference between the long-term and short-term memory. **(4 marks)**

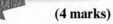

Visual and verbal guidance

Different types of **guidance** can be used to help performers improve. The type of guidance used depends on the skill and the ability of the performer. You need to be able to choose and justify which type of guidance is most appropriate for beginners or elite performers and be able to give examples of how the guidance can be given.

Visual guidance (seeing)

Visual guidance is when the performer is shown the skill. This can be done in a variety of ways, for example:

- a video of the performer
- pictures (e.g. photos or sketches)
- a good-quality demonstration.

When using visual guidance:

- images must be clear (to enable understanding)
- demonstrations must be seen more than once (so the movement can be remembered)
- demonstrations must be good quality (so poor movement is not copied)
- demonstrations must be clearly visible.

Visual guidance is good for beginners so they can see what the skill should look like and create a mental image of what the movement should be.

It is also used when it is not possible to hear verbal guidance, for example, during play.

Advantages:

👍 performer can copy the movement

👍 can be used with groups

Disadvantages:

👎 if demonstration is poor, incorrect movement can be learned

👎 time-consuming/expensive if video used

👎 as complex or quick movements are difficult to see clearly, can be difficult to recognise what the action is and to copy it

Verbal guidance (hearing)

Verbal guidance is when the performer is told information about how to complete the correct technique.

When using verbal guidance:

- the information must be clear (so the meaning is understood)
- the information must be concise (too much information can be confusing)
- the performer must be able to hear the instruction.

Golden rule

A combination of types of guidance can be used, such as giving both visual and verbal guidance so the performer can see what the movement should look like while being told how to do it.

Verbal guidance is good for more experienced performers who know what the movement should look like and can make sense of the information. It is also used in situations where demonstrations are not possible, for example, during a break in play.

Advantages:

👍 instructions can be given quickly

👍 can be used during performance

👍 no equipment required

Disadvantages:

👎 some movements are hard to explain

👎 relies on the coach's communication skills being good enough so that the performer can understand the information

Worked example

State **one** disadvantage of verbal guidance.

(1 mark)

Verbal guidance can be confusing if too much information is given.

Now try this

During a coaching session the performers are shown a picture of how to hold a golf club.

State the type of guidance being used and the likely level of ability of the group. **(2 marks)**

Manual and mechanical guidance

The two other types of guidance you need to know are manual and mechanical.

Manual guidance

Manual guidance is where the coach physically supports or moves the performer to help them get into the correct position.

Examples include:

- a tennis coach holding a performer's racket arm and moving it through the correct range of motion for a forehand drive
- a trampoline coach supporting a front somersault.

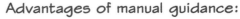

Manual guidance: a gymnastics coach supporting a handstand

Advantages of manual guidance:

👍 performer can get a feel for the movement

👍 builds confidence

👍 can help break down a movement into phases

Disadvantages of manual guidance:

👎 feeling is not the same as actually doing it unaided

👎 performer can become dependent on the support

👎 incorrect feel can lead to incorrect movement being learned

👎 can only be used 1:1

Mechanical guidance

Mechanical guidance is where the coach uses equipment to support the performer to help them with the technique. For example:

- using a harness when learning somersaults in trampolining.

Mechanical guidance: using floats when learning leg movements in swimming

Mechanical guidance can be used when the situation is dangerous.

Advantages:

👍 performer can get a feel for the movement

👍 builds confidence

👍 reduces danger

Disadvantages:

👎 feeling is not the same as actually doing it unaided

👎 performer can become dependent on the support

👎 incorrect feel can lead to incorrect movement being learned

👎 cannot normally be used with large groups

Worked example

Using an example, explain why mechanical guidance might lead to the performer becoming dependent on the support. **(3 marks)**

Mechanical guidance uses equipment; if a performer learns to swim using a float they may become reliant on it and not have the confidence to be in the water without the float.

Now try this

Which option uses manual guidance? **(1 mark)**

A Performers are told how to complete the skill ☐
B Performers are shown how to complete the skill ☐
C Performers are supported completing the skill ☐
D Equipment is used to learn the skill ☐

Remember: **explain** means to show your knowledge and understanding of the topic and then apply it.

Types of feedback

Feedback is used to help improve skill. You need to know what each type of feedback involves and be able to select and justify the appropriate type of feedback for beginners and elite performers.

Intrinsic feedback

Intrinsic feedback is from **within** the performer, for example, how the movement felt from feedback from the muscles. This type of feedback is important so performers can learn to spot their own errors.

Intrinsic feedback should be developed so the performer is not too reliant on others. Experienced performers use intrinsic feedback as:

- the skill is already well learned
- they can feel their own errors and make amendments to their own performance based on their internal feedback.

Extrinsic feedback

Extrinsic feedback is feedback from **outside** the performer, for example, feedback from the coach telling you what you did right or wrong.

Extrinsic feedback is important, as someone watching the skill can observe problems and explain what needs to be done to correct them.

Less experienced performers are more likely to need extrinsic feedback, as they are not yet able to detect their own errors.

Knowledge of results

This focuses on whether your performance got the result you wanted, for example:

- Did you run 100m in 14 seconds?
- Did your serve land where you intended?

It is useful for beginners, to see how near they are to achieving the result they want.

The focus can then be on what needs to be done to achieve the desired result, which can be applied though knowledge of performance.

Knowledge of performance

This focuses on the way you carried out the skill or technique, for example:

- Was your sprint start technique correct?
- Were you using the correct grip when you served?

It is useful for more advanced performers, to determine what needs to be done to improve the technique, leading to improved results.

Positive feedback

- Being told what was **good about** your performance or technique.
- More motivating for beginners, as being told they did something wrong can cause demotivation.

Negative feedback

- Telling you what **was wrong** with your performance or technique.
- Used with more experienced performers who can use this information to correct errors in technique.

Worked example

Explain why beginners would not be able to rely on intrinsic feedback when performing a skill. **(3 marks)**

A beginner will not have a clear idea of the skill they are trying to perform, so they will not be able to feel whether they are doing the movement right or wrong. They will therefore need extrinsic feedback from a coach.

Now try this

 Use of data The graph shows level of success at completing a skill over a number of attempts.

Analyse the graph to consider how feedback may account for the changing level of success. **(4 marks)**

The inverted-U theory

You need to be able to describe the inverted-U theory and be able to draw and correctly label an inverted-U graph. In addition, you need to know how optimum **arousal** levels vary according to the skill being performed in a physical activity or sport.

The inverted-U theory

This theory states that as arousal increases, so does performance up to an optimum point, after which if arousal continues to rise, performance will drop owing to becoming over anxious.

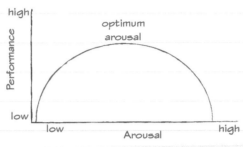

Inverted U-graph showing the relationship between arousal and performance level

Key terms

Arousal: a physical and mental (physiological and psychological) state of alertness or readiness, varying from deep sleep to intense excitement/alertness.

Optimum arousal: the point at which the best, or optimal, performance occurs.

Levels of arousal

The optimum level of arousal will vary depending on the type of **skill** being performed and the level of the performer. For example:

- **Fine movement skills** such as a golf putt, where concentration and precise movement is required, need lower levels of arousal.

- **Gross movement skills** such as a tackle in rugby, where large muscle movements are required, require higher levels of arousal.

- A beginner will need lower levels of arousal.

- An expert will need higher levels of arousal.

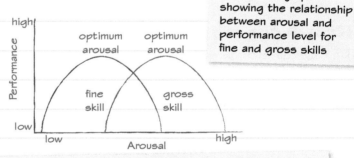

Inverted U-graph showing the relationship between arousal and performance level for fine and gross skills

Any performer who is under or over aroused will experience a drop in performance.

Note the instruction in the question to use 'examples'. As a minimum, make sure your answer has two different examples to illustrate the points you are making. The question also mentions changing levels of arousal, so it is a good idea to mention low, optimum and high levels and how this affects performance in the activities you have used for your examples.

Worked example

Describe, using examples, the effect of changing levels of arousal on performance. **(4 marks)**

At low levels of arousal, performance is normally low. For example, if performing a tackle in rugby with low arousal, the tackle is unlikely to be effective. To be performed well, arousal would need to be higher, but not too high — it would have to be at an optimum level. All skills have an optimum level of arousal, for example a golf putt. If arousal is too high the golfer is more likely to miss their shot.

Now try this

Draw and label an inverted-U graph. **(3 marks)**

Remember: when asked to draw and label a graph, make sure you clearly label both the x-axis and the y-axis.

Stress management 1

You need to know how arousal can be controlled using stress management techniques and be able to explain how these techniques are carried out, using sporting examples.

How arousal can be controlled

- Correct levels of arousal are key to good performance.
- As well as being under aroused (not alert and not ready to perform your best), you can become over aroused and over anxious, causing you to go over your optimum; your performance then drops.
- Stress management techniques can be used before or during performance to help control anxiety levels, so maintaining the level of performance.
- Relaxation techniques include mental rehearsal and visualisation/imagery. These involve control of mental thoughts and imagining positive outcomes.

Mental rehearsal

Mental rehearsal is a technique used by many elite performers. It involves mentally practising a skill or movement before physically doing it.

- During a warm up, you prepare physically and mentally for the coming activity. Mental preparation can be through mental rehearsal.
  For more on the phases of a warm up, see page 63.
- During an event, the performer goes through a skill or sequence of events they are about to perform in their mind. This helps clarify the skill they are about to perform, so they are confident they are ready to perform.

Visualisation/imagery

The use of imagery can be completed in different ways, for example:

- You visualise yourself playing well with a successful outcome.
- You visualise yourself in a comfortable, stress-free environment and focus on how relaxed you feel in that imagined environment.

Focusing on these positive images helps reduce over arousal, so that optimum performance levels can be achieved.

Before participating in the Winter Olympics, this luge performer will mentally go through the race, visualising their route down the track before actually racing. This helps them to be mentally prepared for each twist and turn on the way down.

Worked example

Albert is competing in an important gymnastic competition. He completes his warm up but then has to wait before he can complete the vault. As he waits he starts to lose concentration and confidence, noticing the audience noise and worrying about the importance of this vault. Explain **one** technique Albert could use just before his vault to help regain confidence. **(3 marks)**

Albert could use mental rehearsal. Going through the vault he is about to do in his head will help him to focus and forget about the crowd. He will see himself doing the vault well, increasing his confidence.

Now try this

Say what you know about mental rehearsal and then apply this knowledge to the situation.

Figure 1

Before completing the high jump the performer in **Figure 1** uses the technique of mental rehearsal.
Briefly explain why this technique would be beneficial to him. **(3 marks)**

Stress management 2

As well as using visual techniques to help reduce over arousal, there are many others. **Deep breathing** and **positive self-talk** are two other stress management techniques you need to know about.

Deep breathing

- Over arousal can occur before or during a sporting activity.
- Sometimes when you become over aroused your breathing becomes shallower.
- Deep breathing techniques can be used before the activity or at an appropriate time during it to help reduce arousal.
- Concentrating on taking long, deep breaths helps you focus on the breathing technique rather than on what is causing the increased anxiety.

For example: you are just about to take a free throw in basketball.

1 Slow down; focus on breathing in more slowly for longer.

2 Then breathe out more slowly for longer.

3 When you feel less aroused and therefore more calm, take the throw.

Deep breathing is slow, which helps to reduce stress and therefore maintain focus.

Positive self-talk

If you become over aroused and performance starts to drop, it is easy to think negative thoughts about your own performance. If this happens the level of your performance is likely to drop even further. One of the ways to help prevent this is by saying encouraging things to yourself.

Positive self-talk helps to develop more positive feelings about your own performance.

For example: you have just hit the shuttle into the net in badminton. As you get back into position for the next rally, speak positively to yourself.

Examples of positive self-talk are:

- "Come on, you can do this."
- "Be patient, don't rush – you can do it."
- "You know you can beat them."

Using stress management techniques

Stress management techniques are like any other technique you want to improve – they get better with practice. Therefore with practice you can become more successful in reducing arousal and anxiety.

Stress management techniques are not just for reducing anxiety in sporting situations – you can use them to help you whenever you feel anxiety, for example when revising and in exams.

Figure 1   Figure 2

Worked example

Look at the performers in **Figure 1** and **Figure 2**. Explain which performer would be most likely to use a stress management technique before executing the skill shown. **(3 marks)**

The archer, as they will need a lower level of arousal for their sport. If they are over aroused it will be harder to hit the target, whereas the rugby players need high levels of arousal to take part in a scrum.

Now try this

Give an example of the positive self-talk a goalkeeper might use before a penalty shoot-out in football. **(1 mark)**

Aggression

You need to know the difference between **direct** and **indirect aggression** with application to specific sporting examples.

Aggression or not aggression?

Not all forceful acts in sport are aggressive. For example, consider:

- a 50–50 challenge in football that leads to the unintentional injury of an opponent
- an assertive tackle in rugby, where the aim is simply to win the ball, with no intention of hurting an opponent.

Not all physical contact in sport is classed as aggression.

Aggression

An aggressive act in sport:

- is used to **deliberately** cause harm or injure another person; for example, performing a high tackle in rugby
- can be physical or mental, provided the intent is to harm
- can be classified as direct aggression or indirect aggression.

Aggression can be due to a number of reasons, such as frustration because you are not playing at your best or frustration at your opponent because they are preventing you from winning.

Direct aggression

The term **direct aggression** is an aggressive act that **involves physical contact** with others to cause physical harm to gain an advantage.

Aggressive acts are normally outside the rules of the sport, but the player still carries them out in the hope they will not be caught.

Indirect aggression

This is an aggressive act that **does not involve physical contact**. It could be:

- a nasty remark
- an act against an **object** to gain advantage.

The intended harm is mental rather than physical – something to put the opposition off their game.

A hard shot directed straight at an opponent in tennis could intimidate them and keep them at the back of the court, on the defensive.

Worked example

Explain how one of the players in **Figure 1** could use direct aggression while going for the ball to gain an advantage over the other player. **(3 marks)**

One of the players could deliberately elbow the other player as they go up for the ball, hoping they will not be seen and penalised by the referee. The elbowed player would be less likely to head the ball, so the aggressive player could get to the ball and their team gain possession.

Figure 1

Use the image to help answer the question. Note how the answer links to Figure 1.

Now try this

Identify the type of aggression being described:
Aggression taken out on an object to gain advantage

(1 mark)

Personality

You need to know the characteristics of **introvert** and **extrovert** personality types, including examples of sports that suit these particular personality types.

Personality

Your personality is the particular characteristics and behaviours that you generally display.

Your personality can be an indicator of the type of activity you enjoy and choose to take part in. There are always exceptions to this, but it can give a general guideline.

The two types of personality are:
- introvert
- extrovert.

Introvert

A quiet, passive, reserved personality type, usually associated with individual sports performance.

Characteristics of an introvert:
- shy
- quiet
- thoughtful
- enjoy being on their own

Introverts tend to play individual sports that require:
- concentration and precision (fine skill), such as archery
- low arousal, such as running.

Introverts are usually associated with individual activities.

Extrovert

A sociable, active, talkative, outgoing personality type usually associated with team sports players.

Characteristics of an extrovert:
- enjoy interaction with others
- sociable and aroused by others
- enthusiastic and talkative
- prone to boredom when by themselves

Extroverts tend to play team sports where:
- there is a fast pace, such as basketball
- concentration may need to be low
- gross skills are used, such as in rugby (scrum).

Extroverts are usually associated with team games.

Worked example

Match the individuals in **Figure 1** and **Figure 2** to the most appropriate personality type. **(2 marks)**

The boxers are likely to be extroverts. The archer is more likely to be an introvert.

Figure 1

Figure 2

Think about activities' characteristics.
- Are they fast paced?
- Do they involve gross motor skills?
- Is there opportunity to work with others?

If so, the activity is likely to attract players with extrovert personality characteristics.

Now try this

Explain, using examples from both types of sports, **two** reasons why introverts may prefer activities such as archery, compared to team sports. **(4 marks)**

Motivation

You need to be able to define **intrinsic** and **extrinsic** motivation and evaluate the merits of each type of motivation in sport.

What is motivation?

Motivation is:

✓ the drive to succeed

✓ the desire to achieve something

✓ the inspiration to do something.

In sport, we often use the term motivation in relation to whether someone is motivated to train or to try their best.

Different things can motivate us; these can be categorised as either **intrinsic** or **extrinsic** motivation.

Intrinsic motivation

Intrinsic motivation is the drive that comes from **within you**.

It is when you are driven to perform well out of a personal feeling of, for example:

- pride
- self-satisfaction
- accomplishment
- self-worth
- achievement.

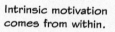
Intrinsic motivation comes from within.

Evaluation of types of motivation

- Any type of motivation is useful.
- Intrinsic motivation is generally thought to be more effective and lead to continued effort, as it doesn't rely on receiving an external reward. If you are only extrinsically motivated and no rewards are available, you may not try your best.
- Receiving extrinsic rewards may lead to feelings of pride and self-satisfaction associated with intrinsic motivation.
- Overuse of extrinsic motivation can reduce intrinsic motivation, as you can become reliant on receiving rewards.

Extrinsic motivation

Extrinsic motivation is the drive to perform well or to win in order to gain **external rewards**, from another source or person. It is when you are driven to perform well for:

- prizes/trophies/medals
- money
- praise.

Winning a medal can be a source of extrinsic motivation for some athletes.

Extrinsic motivation can be divided into:

- **tangible** rewards you can touch, such as certificates, trophies, medals
- **intangible** rewards you can can't touch, such as praise, feedback, applause.

Worked example

In **Figure 1**, Dwayne receives praise from the club manager. Identify the type of motivation and a possible problem if this is the only type of motivation Dwayne receives. **(3 marks)**

Figure 1

Dwayne is receiving praise; therefore, this is extrinsic intangible motivation. If this is the only type of motivation he receives, he may become over-reliant on it and lose motivation if he does not receive praise, leading him to not try as hard when he plays.

Now try this

Name, using examples, **two** types of extrinsic motivation an elite footballer may receive. **(4 marks)**

Social groups: family, friends and peers

You need to know the different social groups, their engagement patterns in physical activity and the factors that affect these groups' participation. This page considers family, friends and peers. The remaining social groups are covered on pages 83–84.

Engagement patterns

Engagement patterns are the general trend of different social groups' participation in physical activity and sport.

The level of participation for each group can be positively or negatively affected by a number of factors.

Some factors can affect any person across the social groups, such as lack of disposable income.

Other factors, however, are more likely to affect certain social groups more than others, such as sexism affecting the gender group.

Family/friends/peers

You can be grouped by those you spend time with. These include:

- parents
- guardians
- relations
- siblings
- friends
- classmates
- other members at sports clubs.

You need to be able to select the most relevant factors affecting participation from the list below and be able to justify your selection.

- attitudes
- **role models**
- accessibility (to facilities/clubs/ activities)
- media coverage
- sexism/stereotyping
- culture/religion/ religious festivals
- family commitments
- available leisure time
- familiarity
- education
- socio-economic/ disposable income
- adaptability/ inclusiveness

Factors affecting engagement patterns

Factors affecting the engagement patterns of the family/friends/peers social group include:

Familiarity: You may do the same activities as other members of your family, for example you play tennis because your Mum plays tennis.

Attitudes: You may not play badminton because, for example, your friends don't like it.

Family commitments: You may not take part in activities owing to, for example, having to look after your younger siblings.

Worked example

Jennifer is a good all-round sports performer and could represent the school in many different sports but has chosen swimming.

State **one** way in which her family may influence her choice of sporting activity. **(1 mark)**

If her family is already involved in certain activities she is likely to try those activities as well and therefore continue with them if she is good and enjoys them.

The key point is that when you are younger, if family members play a particular sport, it is likely that you will go with them and also try the sport. They therefore influence the activities you participate in.

Now try this

The performers pictured are related. Player A is David Beckham, who played at an elite level; player B is his son Brooklyn, who played for a local club.

Explain **one** likely key influence on Brooklyn's choice of activity. **(2 marks)**

Player A

Player B

Gender and age

Engagement patterns in physical activity and sport can differ depending on gender or age.

Gender

Gender groups are determined by a person's sex, which is whether they are male or female.

The reasons men and women participate more or less than each other can be due to:

- the nature of the activity
- the influence of other factors.

Factors affecting gender groups include:

- **Role models**: lack of female role models in many sports
- **Media coverage**: lack of TV coverage of female sports
- **Sexism**: Some girls do not want to play football, as they think others will think them masculine.
- **Stereotyping**: Some men do not want to dance or play netball, as they think these activities are only for females.

Age

People are split into groups based on their age, such as:

- children
- teenagers
- adults
- retirees.

The reasons people from different age groups participate more or less in sport than others can be due to:

- the nature of the activity
- other factors such as 'education' – for example, the school you attend may not offer or have the facilities to play some activities.

Other factors affecting age groups include:

- **Accessibility**: For example, a local tennis club may only allow juniors to play at weekends, and if they have a weekend part-time job this means they cannot play.
- **Disposable income**: Money may be needed to pay bills rather than to pay for sport.
- **Available leisure time**: Some people may have less available time owing to work commitments.
- **Stereotyping**: Some people think you're too old to do sport if you are retired; however, some people in their eighties (and older) still run marathons.

Age does not need to be a barrier to participation in sports such as marathon running.

According to Sport England's Active People Survey, during the period April 2012 to 2013, 54.5 per cent of 16–25 year olds played sport once a week, whereas 34.1 per cent of adults aged 26 years or older played sport once a week.

Identify a relevant factor and state a reason why this factor may account for the different participation rates.

(2 marks)

Available leisure time. Adults may have less time to take part in sport owing to work and family commitments.

Now try this

State **two** factors that could affect the engagement pattern of the social group 'age' and justify your choice.

(4 marks)

83

Race/religion/culture and disability

Engagement patterns in physical activity and sport can differ depending on your ethnic origin or whether you have a disability.

Race/religion/culture

People are grouped based on their culture or specific origin. The reasons people from different ethnic groups participate more or less than other ethnic groups can be due to the nature of the activity or other factors.

Factors for differences in participation include:

- **Cultural influences:** family or peers influencing whether someone does or does not do an activity.
- **Religious festivals** that take precedence over playing sport.

Other factors affecting this group include:

- **Stereotyping:** where people from particular backgrounds are steered towards or away from certain activities; for example, people of African origin being associated with and encouraged to compete in long-distance running events rather than activities such as swimming.
- **Disposable income:** owing to socio-economic grouping, some people from minority groups may have less money; for example, someone without a permanent job would not have the money needed to access many sports.

Disability

Factors for differences in participation include:

- **Adaptability:** There are many adapted activities available for people with disabilities, such as wheelchair tennis and wheelchair rugby. Yet adapting sports is not always possible and can be expensive.
- **Inclusiveness:** Sports facilities may not run sessions for people with disabilities. This means that these facilities are not inclusive of people unable to join in mainstream sporting events.

Other factors affecting this group include:

- **Accessibility:** lack of facilities or clubs as well as physical barriers, such as a lack of ramps or pool hoists.
- **Disposable income:** specialist equipment may be expensive.
- **Stereotyping:** whether by the person with the disability (thinking they are unable to participate) or by others (assuming those with disabilities are unable to take part due to disability).
- Although there has been an increase in **media coverage** of those with disabilities, coverage remains limited and there is a lack of **role models** to aspire to.

Worked example   Use of data

The following data is from the Sports Participation and Ethnicity in England National Survey 1999/2000. This survey gives the participation rates for cricket during this period: Pakistani (10%), 'Black Other' (8%) and Indian (6%) men, which compares with the average for all men of 2%.

Explain **two** factors for the different levels of participation between different ethnic groups. **(4 marks)**

The higher figures for the ethnic group 'Pakistani' could be due to stereotyping, where people have been encouraged to play cricket because of their ethnic origin, or due to cultural influences, whereby friends or family have introduced them to the sport.

Now try this

Paul is a wheelchair user and wants to start to play wheelchair basketball. Describe a potential barrier Paul could face when taking up this sport.

(2 marks)

Commercialisation

You need to know what **commercialisation** is and about the relationship between sport, **sponsorship** and the **media**; in other words, how they all interlink.

What is commercialisation?

Commercialisation is to manage or exploit (an organisation or an activity) in a way designed to make a profit.

Commercial organisations are those that need to make a profit from the sale of goods, services or events. These organisations can use sport to get their product seen by millions, via advertising or sponsorship.

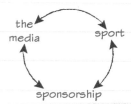

The relationship between sponsorship, sport and the media is essential for each to maximise opportunity and profit, so that everyone benefits.

Sponsorship

A **sponsor** is an individual or group that provides support in the form of sponsorship; in return they can get their product seen by millions.

Sponsorship can be for:

* an **individual**; for example, golfer Rory McIlroy has been sponsored by Nike

* a **team** or **group**; for example, Manchester United FC has been sponsored by Chevrolet

* an **event, activity** or **organisation**; for example, Visa was a main sponsor of the 2012 Olympic Games.

Different types of sponsorship include:

* financial

* clothing and equipment, including footwear

* facilities, such as sports stadia.

Media

Media are diversified (a broad range of) technologies that act as the main means of mass communication. They include:

* printed media/press (such as newspapers)

* broadcast media (such as TV and radio)

* internet/social media (such as Facebook).

Sponsors and the media

* Sponsors want to promote their products via the media, as they can reach millions of potential customers.

* Media companies need high viewing figures to make them more attractive to sponsors.

* Media companies therefore pay sports clubs to allow them to televise matches, as this attracts a lot of viewers, making it more likely that they will get funding from sponsors.

Sport

The player/performer and the sport itself need funding for:

* facilities   * competitions.

* equipment

Both the media and commercialisation can help promote sport, and the media can also provide better opportunities for the spectator.

Worked example

Briefly explain why media providers, for example, Sky or BT Sport, fight to get exclusive rights to televise particular events. **(3 marks)**

Some events are very popular with viewers. Media companies want to be the only ones showing a popular event so that commercial organisations are interested in sponsoring the event or buying 'air time' to advertise their product, as they will be reaching a large number of people.

Now try this

State why commercial organisations, such as the company named on the advertising banners in **Figure 1**, are interested in sponsoring events such as the Olympic Games. **(2 marks)**

Figure 1

The advantages of commercialisation

You need to know the positive impacts of sponsorship and the media and be able to justify why the impact is positive.

Advantages for the sponsor/company

👍 Excellent and relatively inexpensive advertising of their products, as:
  👍 media can show products in advertisements during breaks in play
  👍 brand names can be seen around venues and on performers' clothing during activity.
👍 Raised awareness of brands, leading to increased sales.
👍 Product associated with high-quality performance or health and fitness, giving brand high status.
👍 Increased media hype about an event = greater viewing numbers = more exposure for sponsor's products.

Advantages for the sport

More media coverage leads to:
👍 raised awareness of sport, to help increase participation
👍 higher profile of sport = more commercial interest
👍 increased funding from sponsors, used to:
  👍 run events
  👍 develop grassroot to elite performers
  👍 develop better facilities.

Advantages for the official

👍 Sponsors can provide kit.
👍 Media can support correct decisions.
👍 They are more likely to become role models.

Advantages for the player/performer

👍 Can be paid millions to endorse products.
👍 Can train full-time and not have to work at another job to fund training, so can focus on becoming the best at their sport.
👍 Can receive top-quality products to use to help performance.

Advantages for the audience/spectator

👍 More coverage
👍 Top events
👍 Replays
👍 Red button choice
👍 Player cam
👍 Ability to buy the same clothes and equipment as role models

Worked example

State **two** reasons why performers such as Lewis Hamilton (see **Figure 1**) want sponsorship deals. **(2 marks)**

They will receive a large income from the sponsors in return for advertising the sponsor's products.
They may also receive top-quality products that help their performance.

Figure 1

Formula 1 racing driver Lewis Hamilton is given as an example. Don't worry if you don't know the performer – think about general reasons why it would be good to get sponsorship.

Now try this

Identify why a sponsor would be interested in sponsoring a top performer such as Lewis Hamilton. **(2 marks)**

The disadvantages of commercialisation

You need to know the negative impacts of sponsorship and the media and be able to justify why the impact is negative.

Disadvantages for the sponsor/company

- 👎 The media may not get a high number of viewers.
- 👎 The company doesn't get the amount of exposure they wanted.
- 👎 The player/team doesn't perform well.
- 👎 A player becomes a bad role model owing to cheating, violence (in sport or out), infidelity, racism, etc. Sponsors become linked to these players and the product receives a negative image, making it less popular and reducing sales.

Disadvantages for the sport

- 👎 Clothing and rules are changed to make the game more appealing to viewers.
- 👎 Fixture times and length of season are changed to maximise viewing opportunities.
- 👎 There are breaks in play for advertising purposes.
- 👎 Minority sports are not shown by media leading to a decrease in participation.
- 👎 Minority sports get little media coverage and therefore lack sponsorship.
- 👎 Negative reporting can give the sport a bad reputation.

Disadvantages for the player/performer

- 👎 Event times may make conditions less favourable for performers.
- 👎 Withdrawal of sponsorship can cause financial difficulties.
- 👎 The product may have a bad image or be unethical, giving the performer a bad reputation.
- 👎 Required appearances take time away from training.
- 👎 There may be pressure to win at all costs to keep sponsorship.
- 👎 They are restricted to sponsorship clothing/equipment.
- 👎 They have no privacy.
- 👎 Negative reporting can lose sponsorship.

Disadvantages for the official

- 👎 Under a spotlight all decisions can be replayed, so poor decisions are highlighted, undermining the official.
- 👎 They have to wear the sponsor's logo.

Disadvantages for the audience/spectator

- 👎 The subscription cost for TV sports channels is high.
- 👎 Pay per view means they need to pay again for certain events.
- 👎 The cost of merchandise is high.
- 👎 Minority sports are not shown.
- 👎 Sponsors keep the best tickets for hospitality reasons.

Worked example

Give reasons why the media dictating the start times of an event might be a disadvantage to performers. **(3 marks)**

The media will want the time of the event to be when most people are available to watch it. This may mean that it is during the hottest part of the day or in the evening, which may not be the ideal time for the performer to be at their best.

Now try this

Top cyclist Lance Armstrong (see **Figure 1**) admitted taking performance-enhancing drugs during his career. Briefly explain why this is a disadvantage to his sponsors. **(3 marks)**

Figure 1

The advantages of technology

You need to know, and justify, the positive impacts of technology.

Technology

Advances are being made in technology all the time.

Many types of technology are now used to help improve performance, officiating and the spectator experience.

Technology has an impact on:

- clothing and equipment for players
- timing equipment
- goal line technology
- TV systems
- communication systems.

Advantages to the performer and sport

- 👍 Improved equipment, clothing and footwear for **performance**, such as skin suits to reduce resistance, running blades for disabled athletes, lighter, stronger rackets/golf clubs.
- 👍 Improved equipment, clothing and footwear for **safety**, such as ski helmets.
- 👍 Improved security at venues, such as security cameras, metal detectors.
- 👍 Better facilities, such as velodromes for cycling.
- 👍 Better decisions by officials due to technology support, such as review of replays.
- 👍 Better drug testing, to help prevent cheating.

Advantages for the official

- 👍 Technological support means less chance of errors, for example being able to review replays or use a Television Match Official (TMO) to provide additional help to reach the right decision.
- 👍 Improved timing devices mean more accurate results.
- 👍 Wifi allows for improved communication with, for example, officials and technicians.

Advantages for the sponsor

- 👍 Easier to see logos owing to enhanced viewing quality.
- 👍 More coverage of sports provides more opportunity to see products.
- 👍 Advertising opportunities during breaks on TV.
- 👍 Better standard of play using improved equipment encourages more sales.

Advantages for the audience/spectator

- 👍 Multiple viewing platforms, such as TV, tablet, mobile phone.
- 👍 Better picture and sound, creating a better viewing experience.
- 👍 Interactive options (such as player cam).
- 👍 Increased enjoyment as a result of better performances due to technology.
- 👍 Increased interaction at live games with decisions, for example Hawkeye.

At Wimbledon, Hawkeye allows for better decisions about whether a ball was in or out.

 Worked example

Using an example, outline the advantage of technology to:
- sponsors
- sport.   **(4 marks)**

Because of technology, sport can be viewed on a TV, laptop or mobile phone. This means more people can watch sport, so the sponsor has more exposure, increasing interest or sales in their product. This is good for sport, as this will provide more sponsorship, which means more money for the sport, which can be spent developing future talent or facilities.

Figure 1

 Now try this

Explain **one** positive impact of technology for the performer in **Figure 1**.   **(2 marks)**

The disadvantages of technology

You need to know the negative impacts of technology and be able to justify why the impact is negative.

Disadvantages to the performer and sport

- 👎 The costs of equipment increase.
- 👎 State-of-the-art facilities cost more.
- 👎 Technology can go wrong.
- 👎 Repairs can be expensive.
- 👎 Technology can be inaccurate.
- 👎 The human part of lucky decisions is lost.
- 👎 People can watch at home rather than attend live games, resulting in a loss of gate revenue.
- 👎 Players/sports unable to afford modern technology are at a disadvantage.

Disadvantages for officials

- 👎 They become reliant on technology.
- 👎 Technology can go wrong.
- 👎 Technology highlights errors.
- 👎 Decisions are challenged more owing to loss of respect for officials' judgement.

Advances in technology have led to officials' decisions being challenged more frequently.

Disadvantages for the sponsor

- 👎 They need to provide more funding so supported teams/players can:
  - purchase the best equipment to stay at the top of their game (and therefore remain attractive to the sponsor)
  - give players access to the best medical support, such as ice baths or hypoxic tents.
- 👎 Sponsored players may be found cheating, which reflects badly on the sponsor.

Disadvantages for the audience/ spectator

- 👎 Breaks in play waiting for decisions can be boring.
- 👎 The technology changes the nature of the sport.
- 👎 They have to pay to view some sports.
- 👎 They have to pay for specialist sports channels on TV.
- 👎 Technology is expensive, such as 3D TVs.
- 👎 They don't experience the excitement of watching the match live.

Worked example

As shown in **Figure 1**, Hawkeye predicts the trajectory of a ball.
Explain **two** negative impacts of technology such as Hawkeye for a tennis player.

The umpire might have called their shot in, but after the Hawkeye review it could be called out, therefore they would lose the point. Also, your opponent could use Hawkeye to unsettle you; for example, to break your rhythm if you have been playing well and it is at an important part of the match.

Figure 1

Even if you are unsure about the technology, use the image to help you. You can see it is being used to trace the flight of the ball. How might this be a disadvantage to a player?

Now try this

Explain **one** negative impact of technology such as the Television Match Official to sport. **(3 marks)**

Conduct of performers

You need to know the terms used in relation to the conduct of performers and be able to give sporting examples.

Key terms

Etiquette: This is a convention or unwritten rule in an activity. It is not an enforceable rule but it is usually observed. It is basically displaying dignity and good manners in sport.

Contract to compete: This is an unwritten agreement to follow and abide by the written and unwritten rules and to give 100 per cent effort.

Sportsmanship

Sportsmanship is the type of behaviour that you should see in sport. It is where players display good etiquette and abide by the contract to compete. They do not try to win by unfair means. For example:

👍 showing respect for officials and opponents

👍 shaking hands with opponents

👍 kicking the ball out of play if an opponent is injured

👍 being honest if the ball is out or if they break a rule.

Shaking hands before a match is considered a sign of good sportsmanship.

Sportsmanship creates:

👍 good role models

👍 a positive image of the sport or activity

👍 satisfaction/pride – you know you won honestly.

Gamesmanship

Gamesmanship is the type of behaviour that you **should not** see from performers in sport. It is bending (but not breaking) the rules to gain an unfair advantage.

For example:

👎 playing for time if winning

👎 entering a weaker team if the following match is more important

👎 sledging in cricket.

Sledging is when players verbally abuse their opponent to make them lose concentration and play badly.

Gamesmanship creates:

👎 bad role models

👎 a negative image of the sport or activity

👎 dissatisfaction – you know that you won owing to an unfair advantage.

Worked example

State **one** reason why sportsmanship is a better behaviour than gamesmanship. **(2 marks)**

Sportsmanship is better as the players are not trying to win by gaining an unfair advantage, therefore they create a more positive image of their sport.

Remember to use the number of marks available as a guide to how much information you need to give. In this answer, one piece of information is about sportsmanship and this is extended, giving the reason it is good for sporting image.

Now try this

To help remember which behaviour is which: 'a good sport' (as in sportsmanship) is good behaviour.

Figure 1 shows a performer helping a member of the opposition who has cramp. Identify the sporting behaviour being shown. **(1 mark)**

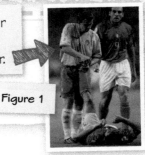

Figure 1

Blood doping

Prohibited substances have been banned as there are dangerous side effects and they can improve performance artificially. The World Anti-Doping Agency (WADA) is responsible for testing for these substances. You need to know the prohibited substances and prohibited methods and their basic positive and negative side effects.

Blood doping

Blood doping is different from taking performance-enhancing drugs (PEDs), as it is a method that is followed rather than something you take. It is a process some athletes will use to enhance their performance. This method, like PEDs, is banned from use in sport.

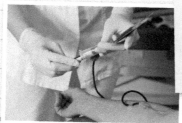
Blood doping is a process where performers have additional blood added to their bloodstream.

How is blood doping done?

Blood doping can be done in a number of ways. The method you need to know is the one below, using the performer's own blood:

1 The performer has their blood removed a few weeks before competition.

2 This blood is frozen and stored.

3 During this time the body replaces the removed blood.

4 Just before competition the performer's stored blood is re-injected into the performer.

Reasons performers dope

- Increase in red blood cells, therefore:
- Increase in oxygen-carrying capacity.

Side effects associated with blood doping

- Infection from equipment or blood contamination during storage, leading to blood poisoning.
- Increased thickness (viscosity) of the blood due to increased number of red blood cells, which could lead to blood clots/heart attack.
- Deep vein thrombosis due to blood clots, leading to heart failure.
- Stroke as a result of blood clots.
- Diseases carried in body fluids, for example, HIV and hepatitis.
- Embolism (blockage of blood vessel).

Who might use blood doping?

Any performer who takes part in an activity where an increase in **oxygen** delivery would be an advantage, such as:

- long-distance cyclists
- long-distance runners
- games players where the game can last hours.

Blood doping can benefit endurance athletes.

Worked example

Use the number of marks available as a guide to the number of points you make.

In an attempt to improve performance, some participants will resort to blood doping. Explain the type of activity these performers are likely to compete in. **(3 marks)**

They are likely to take part in an endurance event such as long-distance running. This is because they are getting extra blood so they can carry more oxygen, which is required to produce energy aerobically, allowing them to maintain a higher level of performance for longer.

Now try this

Explain why blood doping might lead to infection. **(2 marks)**

Beta blockers

You need to know about performance-enhancing drugs (PEDs) and their positive and negative effects on sporting performance. **Beta blockers** should only be prescribed by a medical professional to control medical conditions, not to aid sports performance.

What are beta blockers?

Beta blockers are drugs that are designed to treat various health issues, particularly those associated with the heart such as high blood pressure. They work by blocking the effects of adrenaline, so helping slow down the heart rate.

They improve fine motor control/preciseness

They have a calming effect

They reduce heart rate, muscle tension and blood pressure

Reasons performers might take beta blockers

They reduce the performer's anxiety

They allow the performer to remain in control

They increase the chances of winning

They reduce muscle tremor or shaking

Side effects associated with beta blockers

- Nausea
- Weakness
- Heart problems
- Slowing heart rate (therefore lower oxygen delivery, therefore drop in performance in endurance events)
- Lowering of blood pressure
- Sleep disturbance leading to tiredness

As beta blockers work with chemicals that occur naturally within the body and they are quickly absorbed, it can be hard to detect them when testing for banned drugs.

Who might use beta blockers?

Use of beta blockers could be an advantage in any activity that depends on precision and fine control, such as golf and archery.

Other activities that may be associated with taking beta blockers include:

- target shooting
- gymnastics.

Worked example

Which of the following is a known effect of beta blockers on health? **(1 mark)**

A High blood pressure ☐   C Nausea ⬤

B Dehydration ☐   D Loss of balance ☐

Now try this

Some participants take illegal performance-enhancing drugs to control their heart rate, despite the obvious health risks.

What effect do beta blockers have on a participant's heart rate? **(1 mark)**

 Make sure you read the question carefully. This question asks about the effect on heart rate, so make sure you mention what happens to heart rate in your response.

Stimulants

You need to know about **stimulants** and their positive and negative effects, and be able to give examples of which type of sports performers may decide to use them.

What are stimulants?

Stimulants are a category of drugs that temporarily elevate mood. They increase brain activity, making an individual feel more awake and alert, and as if they have more energy. The taking of stimulants in large enough quantities constitutes the use of performance-enhancing drugs and is therefore banned.

To increase alertness (mental and physical) so the performer is quicker to respond

Reasons performers might take stimulants

To increase levels of aggression

To reduce tiredness

To increase competitiveness

To increase heart rate (and therefore oxygen delivery)

Side effects associated with stimulants

Reported side effects of stimulants include:

- insomnia
- anxiety
- aggression
- heart rate irregularities.

Facts about stimulants

☑ Stimulants are found in everyday products that contain caffeine, for example, coffee and many soft drinks. However, you are unlikely to reach banned levels of caffeine simply through drinking these!

☑ Stimulants can be used to treat anything from a cold to attention deficit hyperactivity disorder (ADHD).

☑ Amphetamines are one of the most common stimulants that are used illegally.

Who might use stimulants?

There are two main areas where stimulants might appeal to performers.

1 Where an increase in **aggression** would be helpful; it helps to have a certain level of aggression in very physical sports as the performer is more prepared to take the 'physical knocks', for example in:

- rugby
- boxing
- ice hockey.

2 Where the performer needs to stay **alert** over a long period of time, for example in:

- long-distance cycling
- baseball.

Worked example

Which of the following is a side effect of stimulants?   **(1 mark)**
A Nausea and vomiting   ⊖   C Irregular and increased heart rate   ⬤
B Dehydration   ⊖   D Loss of balance   ⊖

Consider all options and make sure your choice is the best from those available.

Now try this

Describe the circumstances that might lead to a performer taking stimulants, even though they are a banned performance-enhancing drug.
(2 marks)

Narcotic analgesics

You need to know about **narcotic analgesics** and their positive and negative effects, and be able to give examples of which type of sports performers may decide to use them.

Narcotic analgesics were designed to relieve pain temporarily. They act on the brain and spinal cord to dampen the effect of painful stimuli, thus masking pain.

They increase the performer's pain threshold

They give a sense of euphoria

Reasons performers might take narcotic analgesics

They mask injuries so the performer can continue to compete

They give a sense of being invincible

Side effects associated with narcotic analgesics

Reported side effects include:

- nausea/vomiting
- anxiety/depression
- kidney/liver damage
- addiction
- concentration loss
- further damage to injury (due to masking pain).

Who might use narcotic analgesics?

Activities where performers might risk using narcotic analgesics include:

- sprinting
- boxing
- football
- swimming.

Any performer who overtrains may take them as painkillers.

Worked example

When might a performer be tempted to take narcotic analgesics? **(1 mark)**

When they have an injury but need to continue to train.

Now try this

When injured, some performers may be tempted to take drugs to allow them to maintain their training.

What category of drug would a performer take to mask or hide pain? **(1 mark)**

 Make sure you know the reasons why performers are tempted to take performance-enhancing drugs.

Anabolic agents

Anabolic agents are those that help develop muscle mass such as **anabolic steroids**. You need to know about anabolic agents and their positive and negative effects, and be able to give examples of which type of sports performers may decide to use them.

Why use anabolic agents?

Many types of anabolic steroids have the same chemical structure as the male hormone testosterone. This is produced naturally by the body, but performers increase the amount they have by taking artificially produced versions of it.

To allow them to train harder for longer, so increasing **power** and **strength**

To increase protein synthesis, helping to **develop lean muscle mass**

Reasons athletes take anabolic steroids

To increase their chances of winning

To speed up recovery time

Owing to pressure from others

Side effects associated with anabolic agents

There are lots of good reasons **not** to take performance-enhancing drugs (PEDs). Using PEDs in competition is **cheating**.

There are also significant health risks, including:

* liver damage and coronary heart disease
* testicular atrophy, which leads to a decrease in sperm count (infertility)
* skin problems, including acne
* mood swings, including increased aggression
* premature baldness.

Who might use anabolic agents?

Anabolic steroids could provide an advantage in activities requiring **power**, like sprinting or weightlifting.

Sprinter Tyson Gay was banned from competing in 2013 after testing positive for anabolic steroids.

Worked example

Rank these performers in order, so that the one most likely to use anabolic steroids is listed first, and the one least likely is listed last. **(1 mark)**

* Tennis player
* Long-distance runner
* Sprinter

Sprinter, tennis player, long-distance runner

This rank order is based on the relative importance of power and strength to each of the performers. The more important they are, the more 'attractive' taking steroids becomes.

Now try this

Identify **two** possible side effects of taking anabolic steroids. **(2 marks)**

EXAM ALERT!

Remember to give **two** side effects. Students sometimes make the mistake of giving only one side effect. Make sure you answer the question.

Diuretics

You need to know about **diuretics** and their positive and negative effects, and be able to give examples of which type of sports performers may decide to use them.

What are diuretics?

Diuretics are drugs that increase the rate of urination, so increasing the amount of fluid the body loses. Unlike other performance-enhancing drugs, diuretics are banned not because they directly enhance performance, but because of other potential benefits.

To achieve quick weight loss (due to loss of fluid from the body)

Reasons performers might take diuretics

To mask or hide other performance-enhancing substances the performer may have taken, making them harder to detect

Side effects associated with diuretics

Reported side effects of diuretics include:

- dehydration
- nausea, headaches
- heart/kidney failure.

Golden rule

If you are asked about the side effects of drugs, don't refer to 'heart problems' or 'kidney problems', as these are too vague.

Who might use diuretics?

Diuretic use could be an advantage in any activity with a weight category or where it is a benefit to be light, for example horse racing (jockey) and boxing.

Diuretics could also be useful to any performer trying to mask other performance-enhancing drugs.

Worked example

Give an example of a performer who may take diuretics in order to achieve quick (but temporary) weight loss.   **(1 mark)**

Boxer

Boxers have to be within certain weight categories before they are allowed to compete.

EXAM ALERT!

Do give the obvious answer – make sure you focus on what's being asked and don't overcomplicate your answer.

Now try this

Which of these categories of drugs is used to hide the presence of other performance-enhancing drugs?   **(1 mark)**

A Anabolic steroids ⬭   C Diuretics ⬭

B Stimulants ⬭   D Narcotic analgesics ⬭

You may be able to answer some multiple choice questions without looking at the options given. Even if you know the answer to the question, looking at the other options is a good way of checking your answer.

Peptide hormones

You need to know about **peptide hormones** and their positive and negative effects, and be able to give examples of which types of sports performers may decide to use them. Peptide hormones are a type of performance-enhancing drug (PED) and are found naturally in the human body. Some performers are tempted to increase the amount of these hormones artificially to gain benefits.

Peptide hormones

Two common peptide hormones are:

- **Erythropoietin (EPO)**
  EPO is one occasion where you can write an abbreviation in your exam paper!
- **Human growth hormones (HGH)**
  You will sometimes see the abbreviation HGH – this stands for human growth hormones.

Reasons performers might take peptide hormones

EPO can:

- help increase red blood cell production, and therefore:
- increase oxygen delivery to working muscles.

HGH can:

- help increase muscle mass and therefore strength
- burn more fat.

Side effects associated with peptide hormones

Reported side effects of peptide hormones include:

EPO

- increased thickness of the blood
- blood clots/strokes/deep vein thrombosis
- increased risk of heart attack.

HGH

- arthritis
- heart failure
- abnormal growth in feet and hands
- diabetes.

Who might use peptide hormones?

Activities where performers might risk using peptide hormones include:

EPO

Any activity where an increase in **oxygen** delivery would be helpful, for example:

- rugby
- distance running
- distance cycling.

HGH

Any activity where an increase in **strength** would be helpful, for example:

- sprinting
- weightlifting.

Worked example

In an attempt to improve performance, some participants will resort to taking performance-enhancing drugs. If a performer takes erythropoietin (EPO), what type of activity are they likely to compete in?   **(1 mark)**

An endurance event like long-distance running.

Now try this

Explain how erythropoietin (EPO) aids performance in long-distance runners.   **(3 marks)**

Pros and cons of taking PEDs

Unfortunately sometimes performers do resort to taking performance-enhancing drugs (PEDs). You need to know the advantages and disadvantages to the performer and the sport/event.

The advantages to the performer of taking PEDs

👍 **Increased chances of success**: For example, an archer taking beta blockers to reduce tremble may be more accurate.

👍 **Fame**: The more successful you are, the more famous you can become owing to more publicity.

👍 **Wealth**: You get more prize money or sponsorship deals owing to increased success.

👍 **Level playing field**: If everyone were to take them it would make things equal for all performers.

The disadvantages to the sport/ event when performers take PEDs

The sport or event will be associated with cheating, which may give it:

👎 **a bad reputation**: it maynot be given the status or respect it deserves

👎 **poor credibility**: it may be seen as untrustworthy or unreliable.

When performers are found to be taking PEDs there can be a negative effect not only on specific sports and events but also sport as a whole, as some will think that all sports performers will cheat to win.

The disadvantages for the performer of taking PEDs

👎 **Cheating/immoral**: If caught, everyone will know you cheated.

👎 **Associated health risks**: For example, taking EPO increases the risk of blood clots.

👎 **Fines**: If caught, you may need to pay an expensive fine.

👎 **Bans**: For example, you may not be able to compete in the next Olympic games; this may mean that by the time you are allowed to compete again you will be past your peak performance.

👎 **Reputational damage**:

You may, for example:

👎 be publicly shamed by having your medals taken away. For example, Russian Sergey Kirdyapkin was stripped of his gold medal for the 50k walk in the 2012 Olympics after proving positive for a banned substance.

👎 be unable to get sponsorship, as companies will not want their product associated with a cheat. For example, the cyclist Lance Armstrong lost sponsorship deals with Nike after it was discovered he had taken PEDs.

Worked example

The table shows past Olympic doping cases by sport. Explain why it is a disadvantage for a sport to appear on the table. **(2 marks)**

The sport will be associated with cheating and therefore will get a bad reputation.

Number of doping cases reported	Past Olympic doping cases by sport
36	Weightlifting
28	Athletics (track and field)
12	Cross-country skiing
5	Cycling

Now try this

Explain, using an example, why an elite performer might resort to cheating, despite the consequences if caught.

(2 marks)

Always remember to include an example if the question asks for one. Also, don't forget to tailor your answer to the question context. Try to use any images to help you – for example, why would drugs be linked to a gold medal?

Spectator behaviour

You need to know how the behaviour of spectators at live games and events can affect the performers, other spectators and the environment around them.

Advantages of spectators

👍 **Creation of atmosphere**: A large crowd creates excitement, interest and enjoyment, as the players are more motivated and there is interaction among fans. The more positive the experience the more fans will want to attend, raising the income and profile of the sport or event, leading to increased participation.

👍 **Home-field advantage**: Teams and individual performers can gain an advantage from being in familiar surroundings, with fan support and referee bias (where the referee might make decisions in your favour). When the majority of the spectators are cheering for you, you feel lifted by their support and so you play better.

Disadvantages of spectators

👎 **Increased pressure**: For a performer, knowing that the audience really wants your team to win can increase anxiety levels. This can cause the player to become over aroused and their performance level to drop.

👎 **Safety costs/concerns**: It is expensive to employ security staff and security equipment, and to repair damage caused by audience behaviour.

👎 **Negative effect on participation numbers among younger performers**: The poor reputation of a sport, due to audience behaviour, can cause a drop in the number of younger people interested and therefore a loss of potential elite performers.

👎 **Potential for crowd trouble/hooliganism**: Hooliganism may stop real fans attending owing to potential for harm, leading to loss of ticket sales, support and sponsorship.

Reasons for hooliganism

- Rivalries (such as a local derby)
- Hype (from media)
- Fuelled by alcohol/drugs
- Gang culture
- Frustration (at official's decisions, for example)
- Displays of **masculinity**

Strategies to prevent hooliganism

- **Bans**: hooligans banned from travelling abroad or attending matches; teams banned from playing.
- **Fines**: for supporters or clubs.
- **Prison**: for damage to others or property.
- **Increased security**: e.g. CCTV, metal detectors.
- **Segregation**: seating opposing team supporters in separate areas for matches.
- **Early kick-offs**: to prevent drinking of alcohol.
- **All-seater stadia**: more orderly if seated.
- **Alcohol restrictions**: such as none at venues.
- **Education**: promotional campaigns.

Worked example

The referee in **Figure 1** has just issued a red card. State why this might lead to hooliganism.

(2 marks)

Figure 1

The supporters may feel it is the wrong decision and be frustrated by the referee's action.

Now try this

Explain **one** positive influence of spectators at live games and events. **(2 marks)**

Physical health and fitness

You need to know that participation in physical activity and exercise can be linked to an increase in health, well-being and fitness, and how exercise can suit the varying needs of different people.

Physical health and well-being

To have good **physical health and well-being** means:

👍 all of your body systems are working well

👍 you are free from illness and injury

👍 you are able to carry out everyday tasks.

Some people exercise to improve their health and some to improve their fitness.

Regular exercise can provide benefits, so improvements can be made to your **physical health** and **well-being**. These include the following:

1 **Improved heart function**: stronger heart muscle means it pumps more efficiently ➡ Less strain on the heart, reducing the chance of heart attacks

2 **Improved efficiency of body systems**: muscular, skeletal and cardiovascular systems are more efficient; for example weight-bearing activities such as jogging improve the skeletal system ➡ Improves bone density, making bones stronger therefore reducing the chance of osteoporosis

3 **Reduced the risk of some illness**: for example, exercise can reduce high blood pressure ➡ Less chance of coronary heart disease or strokes

4 **Ability to do everyday tasks**: due to improved body systems ➡ Can function more easily at work and leisure, can run for the bus/play sport

5 **Avoidance of obesity**: being very overweight can cause health problems, affecting your participation in sport and ability to carry out everyday tasks ➡ Exercise burns calories, so you are not slowed down by excess weight during sport; also helps reduce health problems associated with obesity, such as heart disease or diabetes

Fitness

Regular exercise can provide benefits, so improving your **fitness**. These include:

1 **improved fitness**: components of fitness can be improved through exercise ➡ Leading to better performance

2 **reduced chances of injury**: due to stronger bones and muscles, and increased flexibility ➡ Meaning more time can be spent training/performing

3 **Supporting physical ability to work**: due to improved fitness components such as strength and muscular endurance ➡ Meaning coping better at work, for example a hairdresser who has to stand for long periods

---

Worked example

Which of the following statements describes a physical health benefit of exercise? **(1 mark)**

A Meeting new people ⬭

B Gaining an aesthetic appreciation of movement ⬭

C Feeling better about body shape ⬭

D Losing weight if overweight ⬤

Now try this

Use an example to explain how poor physical health can affect performance in physical activity.
(3 marks)

Mental (emotional) health

You need to know that in addition to improving physical health, regular physical activity can also improve mental (emotional) health.

Exercise and mental health

The benefits of exercise to **mental health and well-being** include:

1 **reduced stress/tension:** by taking your mind off any problems while you exercise

➡ Helps to prevent stress-related illnesses such as depression

2 **an increase in serotonin:** a chemical found in the body; sometimes also referred to as 'feel good hormones'

➡ When serotonin is released it makes you feel good

3 **greater ability to control emotions:** owing to discipline of doing so when playing sport

➡ Increases confidence and self-esteem

Increase in self-confidence/self-esteem

Another emotional health benefit of exercise is an increase in self-confidence/self-esteem.

Confidence is increased **because:**
• you feel part of something
• you are performing better.

Confidence is increased **by:**
• becoming a member of a team
• practising more.

> **Golden rule**
>
> You should always try to match a reason **why** something is achieved with an example of **how** it can be achieved. Always try to match a 'why' with a 'how'.

Definition of mental health and well-being

The World Health Organization (WHO) defines mental health and well-being as:

"A state of well-being in which every individual:
☑ realises his or her own potential
☑ can cope with the normal stresses of life
☑ can work productively and fruitfully
☑ is able to make a contribution to her or his community."

Mental health and well-being works in conjunction with physical and social health.

Worked example

Physical activity can improve your mental (emotional) health by helping you 'feel good'. Which of the following causes this 'feel good factor'? **(1 mark)**
A An increase in testosterone ☐
B An increase in serotonin ●
C An increase in blood pressure ☐
D An increase in narcotic analgesics ☐

Now try this

One of the possible benefits of an active lifestyle is an increase in **self-esteem**. Using an example, explain how self-esteem can be increased through physical activity. **(3 marks)**

Think about a specific aspect of playing sport and extend this example to make the link to how it can make you feel better about yourself.

Social health

It is important to have *good* **social health and well-being** as well as physical and mental health. Someone who is socially healthy can make friends easily and work well with others.

Friendships and social mixing

Joining a club or team is a great way to achieve the social benefits of exercise. These include:

- 👍 meeting new people and making new friends
- 👍 opportunities to get together with existing friends
- 👍 improving cooperation skills
- 👍 increased social activities (and therefore reduced risk of engaging in antisocial behaviour).

Different age groups

Social benefits of an active lifestyle may well vary between different age groups.

For example, consider the benefits for:

- 👍 an elderly person: getting together with friends as otherwise they may be lonely
- 👍 a child: may see friends at school but needs to develop social skills.

Always be sure to relate your answer to a particular age range if asked to do so.

The importance of cooperating

Cooperation occurs when we work with others and demonstrate teamwork.

Improved co-operation can lead to better understanding of your teammates and better teamwork skills. This may make your team more successful.

Golden rule

Some words are similar, like cooperation, competition and coordination. Don't rush! Always read questions carefully to make sure you are thinking about the right word.

Worked example

Shaznay has lost contact with a lot of her friends since leaving school. She has decided to join a local badminton club.

Explain how joining a club could improve Shaznay's social health. **(3 marks)**

If Shaznay has lost contact with friends, her social health could be negatively affected, as she doesn't have any friends to socialise with. By joining a club she has the chance to make new friends and is less likely to feel lonely, improving her social health.

The question asks you to **explain**. Notice how the first part of the answer identifies Shaznay's problem based on the scenario in the question, while the second part demonstrates **how** joining a sports club will help solve the problem.

Key term

Social health and well-being: This is when basic human needs are met (food, shelter and clothing). The individual has friendship and support, some value in society, is socially active and has little stress in social circumstances. It works in conjunction with physical and mental health.

Now try this

Think carefully about the category!

Enjoyment is a mental benefit of participation in physical activity.
Explain how the social benefits of participation can lead to increased enjoyment. **(2 marks)**

Sedentary lifestyle

You need to be able to define what is meant by a **sedentary lifestyle** and to know the consequences of a sedentary lifestyle on health.

A sedentary lifestyle

A sedentary lifestyle is a lifestyle where there is very limited or no physical activity.

More and more people have sedentary lifestyles owing to advances in technology, as the requirement to be active has reduced. For example, rather than walking or cycling people use cars or public transport to get around. More and more jobs are computer based and therefore sedentary, for example, office work.

The lack of movement is made worse owing to the amount of time spent sitting.

Too much sitting, not enough standing

Even if we are sedentary, research has shown that standing is a better alternative to sitting. It was reported that British people sit for nearly 9 hours (on average) a day.

- ✓ At school and work, large amounts of time are spent sitting down.
- ✓ At home, people spend many hours sitting watching TV or playing computer games.

There is even a campaign called 'Get Britain Standing', to help raise awareness of the need to avoid sitting for prolonged periods of time.

Examples of health risks due to a sedentary lifestyle	Examples of possible causes
Obesity/excessive weight gain	Reduced metabolic rate and inactivity can lead to weight gain.
Heart disease	Risk factors including high blood pressure and increased blood cholesterol can lead to heart disease.
Hypertension (high blood pressure)	Lack of exercise and a poor diet lead to an inefficient heart and potentially damaged blood vessels.
Type 2 diabetes	There is an increased risk of diabetes due to being overweight.
Poor sleep	Lack of oxygen delivery to cells and excessive weight have been linked to snoring and restless legs. This disturbs sleep, as does not doing enough activity to feel tired at night.
Poor self-esteem	Depression can be caused by being overweight, a drop in brain function and low release of serotonin.
Lethargy (lacking in energy)	Low oxygen levels can lead to a feeling of fatigue.

Worked example

 Use of data

The graph shows the percentage of overweight children by age group over a 20-year period. Analyse the data to determine patterns in obesity levels. **(3 marks)**

All you need to know will be shown in the graph, so look carefully and say what you see.

The 11- to 15-year-olds have the highest obesity levels overall, and their percentage shows a continuing, although slight, upward trend. 6- to 10-year-olds showed a slight drop in obesity levels between 2012 and 2013, therefore there is a downward trend for this age group. This is good because in 1994 to 2003 the percentage increase for this age group matched the most overweight group, the 11- to 15-year-olds.

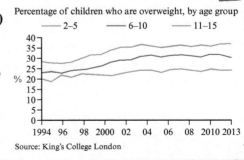

Percentage of children who are overweight, by age group
— 2–5   — 6–10   — 11–15

Source: King's College London

Now try this

Remember to make one point and then expand on it rather than making three unrelated statements.

Give an example of a sedentary lifestyle choice and briefly explain a potential health problem due to this type of lifestyle.

(3 marks)

Obesity

You need to know the definition of **obesity** and how being obese may affect all aspects of health and performance in physical activity and sport.

Key terms

Obesity: this term is used to describe people with a large fat content, caused by an imbalance of calories consumed compared to energy expenditure. A person is considered obese if they have a body mass index (BMI) of over 30, or over 20 per cent above standard weight for height ratio.

This is where the body fat has increased to a level that is seriously unhealthy (*not just being a few pounds overweight*).

Ill health: this refers to being in a state of poor physical, mental and/or social well-being.

How obesity can affect performance

Obesity can adversely affect performance in physical activity and sport. For example:

- 👎 **Limits cardiovascular endurance**: unable to exercise without stopping repeatedly for a period of time, owing to the additional difficulty of carrying a lot of excess weight, and drop in efficiency of the cardio-respiratory system.
- 👎 **Limits flexibility**: excess fat around joints can reduce mobility.
- 👎 **Limits agility**: excess weight makes it harder to change direction quickly.
- 👎 **Limits speed/power**: unable to move fast owing to carrying excess weight.

Obesity can cause ill health (physical)

For example, excess fat has been linked to:

- different types of cancer
- heart disease/heart attacks
- type 2 diabetes
- high cholesterol levels.

Obesity can cause ill health (mental)

For example:

- **Depression**: due to low self-esteem
- **Loss of confidence**: due to perception of what others might think

Obesity can cause ill health (social)

For example:

- **Inability to socialise**: due to loss of confidence, or being housebound
- **Inability to leave home**: due to mobility issues and lack of confidence

Golden rule

Remember, where possible: always try to give reasons to support your examples.

Worked example

Explain how obesity could have an impact on a named component of fitness. **(3 marks)**

A sedentary lifestyle would lead to a drop in cardiovascular endurance due to loss in the efficiency of the heart, making it harder to circulate enough oxygen for prolonged exercise.

Notice how the answer includes a specific 'named' component of fitness. Your answer could have related to a different component of fitness, for example, agility or speed, provided you could explain how obesity would affect it.

Now try this

1. Identify **two** physical health risks associated with being obese. **(2 marks)**
2. Briefly explain **one** impact of being obese on achieving sustained involvement in physical activity. **(3 marks)**

Somatotypes: mesomorphs

There are three extreme body types. The classification of different body types is known as somatotyping. You need to be able to describe the different somatotypes and explain the effect each can have on participation and performance.

Somatotypes

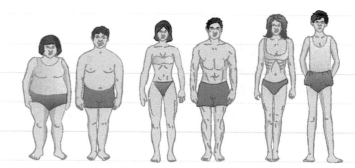

- This is the term used for describing different body types or an individual's physical build.
- It is generally thought that having a certain body type makes you more suited to some activities than others.
- There are three extreme body types:
  - **mesomorph**
  - **ectomorph**
  - **endomorph**.

You only need to know these three categories of somatotypes. Most people are actually somewhere in between these extreme body types.

Mesomorph

Key characteristics are:

- low levels of fat
- builds muscle easily
- solid build
- wide shoulders
- narrow hips.

Individuals with an extreme mesomorph body type are suited to activities requiring power, speed or strength, for example:

- sprinting
- weightlifting
- boxing.

Worked example

Identify the body type of the performer in **Figure 1**.   **(1 mark)**

Mesomorph

This performer needs power to compete their event. For power, you need to be muscular, so a mesomorph body type is an advantage in sprinting.

Figure 1

Now try this

1 State **one** reason why a mesomorph body type is an advantage in tennis.   **(1 mark)**

2 Other than sprinting and playing tennis, identify an activity where having a mesomorph body type would be an advantage.   **(1 mark)**

Somatotypes: ectomorphs and endomorphs

Ectomorphs and endomorphs are two of the three extreme body types you need to know about.

Ectomorph

Key characteristics are:
- long, thin frame
- narrow shoulders and hips
- slim build
- generally does not build muscle easily
- generally does not store fat easily.

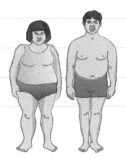

Individuals with an extreme ectomorph body type are suited to activities where being light is an advantage, as there is not too much weight to carry or lift, for example:

- long-distance running
- high jump.

A high jumper will also benefit from being tall.

Endomorph

Key characteristics are:
- wide hips
- narrow shoulders
- has a tendency to store fat.

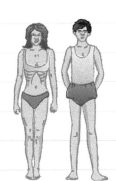

Individuals with an extreme endomorph body type are suited to some activities requiring power or where added weight is an advantage.

They can use their bulk to add momentum to throws, or can overpower or resist opponents, for example in:
- shot put
- sumo wrestling
- some positions in rugby (such as props).

Worked example

Identify the body type of the performer in **Figure 1**.   (1 mark)

Ectomorph

It is an advantage for anyone who needs to lift their own body weight in their event, to be relatively light. The ectomorph body type is therefore well-suited to high jumping.

Figure 1

Now try this

1   Give an example of when an endomorph body type would be an advantage in physical activity.   **(1 mark)**
2   Explain the effect on performance in long-distance running of having an endomorph body type.   **(3 marks)**

Balanced diet and energy use

You need to know how energy is measured and the reasons for having a **balanced diet**.

Explaining a balanced diet

- A balanced diet means eating the right foods, in the right amounts. This will enable you to work and exercise properly.
- Insufficient nutrients can cause health issues, such as anaemia, rickets and scurvy.
- No single food contains all of the nutrients the body needs, so you need to eat a variety of foods in the correct proportions.

Reasons for a balanced diet

1 If the correct amount of calories (energy) is not used, it is stored as fat. This can lead to obesity (particularly saturated fat).

2 The body needs the right nutrient balance for:
- energy for physical activity
- growth
- adequate hydration.
  Go to page 109 to revise hydration (water balance).

Golden rule

Diet is what we eat on a day-to-day basis and should not be confused with 'being on a diet'.

Measuring energy

Energy is measured in **calories (Kcal)** and is obtained from the food we eat.

The average adult male requires 2500 Kcal per day and the average adult female requires 2000 Kcal per day, depending on:

- **age**: Metabolic rate can slow down as you get older, so you burn fewer calories
- **gender**: Men are generally larger than women so tend to need more calories
- **height**: If you are tall you will need more calories than a shorter person
- **energy expenditure (exercise)**: If you exercise you will need more calories than someone with a sedentary lifestyle.

The energy balance

Energy balance is about making sure the quantity of energy from food we take in relates to how much exercise we do.

- If we eat too much in relation to the amount of activity we do, we will become overweight.
- If we eat too little in relation to the amount of activity we do, we will become underweight.

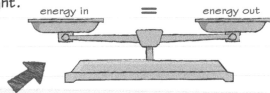
energy in = energy out

We need an energy balance, so we have the correct amount of calories from nutrients for the amount of energy we need.

Worked example

Valentin is trying to improve his diet, to make it more balanced. Define the term 'balanced diet'. **(2 marks)**

Eating different food types to provide suitable nutrients, vitamins and minerals, and eating the right amount of calories for the energy you need, depending on how much you exercise.

Now try this

UK Government guide to calorie intake (www.gov.uk)

 Use of data Using the data in the table, state **two** reasons for the difference in recommended calorie intake for a 16-year-old male and a 51-year-old female. **(2 marks)**

	Age groups (years)										
	7–10		11–14		15–18		19–50		51–64		65–74
	M	F	M	F	M	F	M	F	M	F	M	F
Micronutrients	M	F	M	F	M	F	M	F	M	F	M	F
Energy (Kcal/d)	1970	1740	2220	1845	2755	2110	2550	1940	2465	1900	2330	1900

Nutrition

You need to know the role and importance of **carbohydrates**, **fats**, **proteins**, **vitamins** and **minerals**.

Variety as well as balance

You need:

- a balance of food from the different groups
- a variety from within each group.

For example, we should have a high proportion of fruit and vegetables. It is recommended we eat **a minimum** of '5 a day'.

Variety within portions is important to make sure we get the necessary range of nutrients. This is why eating five apples will only count as one of your '5 a day'. The items we require include:

- carbohydrates
- fats
- protein
- vitamins and minerals.

Carbohydrates

Carbohydrates are:

- the main (and preferred) energy source for all types of exercise, of all intensities (aerobic and anaerobic)
- contained in bread, pasta, potatoes, rice.

A balanced diet should contain: 55%–60% carbohydrate.

Carbohydrates

Fats

Fats

Fats are:

- an energy source: they provide more energy than carbohydrates but only at low intensity
- contained in butter, oil, fatty meats and fried food
- easily stored in the body and can lead to weight gain.

A balanced diet should contain: 25%–30% fat.

Protein

Proteins

Proteins are:

- for growth and repair of muscle tissue
- contained in cheese, milk, eggs, lean meat, fish
- used by performers such as sprinters to aid muscle growth (**hypertrophy**).

A balanced diet should contain: 15%–20% protein.

Vitamins and minerals

Vitamins and minerals are for maintaining the efficient working of the body systems and general health. This includes helping to keep:

- our bones strong
- our immune system working.

Vitamins and minerals

Vitamins are contained in fresh fruit and vegetables. Minerals are contained in lots of different foods, including meat and vegetables.

Worked example

Fats and carbohydrates provide performers with energy.

(a) Which should you eat a larger amount of, fat or carbohydrate? **(1 mark)**

Carbohydrate

(b) Why is this food type a better source of energy for you? **(1 mark)**

It can be used in either aerobic or anaerobic activity.

Now try this

The following should all be present in a balanced diet. Which of them aids bone development? **(1 mark)**

A Fibre ⬭   C Carbohydrates ⬭

B Minerals ⬤   D Protein ⬭

Water balance

You need to know the reasons for maintaining water balance (hydration) and be able to evaluate the consequences of dehydration on performance in different sporting activities.

Key terms

Dehydration: excessive loss of body water, such that it interrupts the function of the body.

Hydration: having enough water to enable normal functioning of the body.

Rehydration: consuming water to restore hydration.

Water balance: refers to taking in water (hydrating) to prevent dehydration due to loss of fluids.

Water balance

When we sweat during physical activity, we lose water and salt. It is vital that the correct levels of these are maintained.

To help avoid dehydration and maintain hydration levels, you need to drink plenty of water or energy drinks:

- two hours before performance
- just before performance
- whenever possible during performance.

Performers drink water after activity to remain hydrated.

Dehydration results in:			Impact on performance
• blood thickening (increased **viscosity**)	→	slows blood flow, therefore oxygen delivery	such as lacking energy to continue running a marathon
• increase in heart rate causing irregular heart rate (rhythm)	→	the heart has to work harder to deliver oxygen to muscles	
• increase in body temperature	→	causes overheating, leading to heat exhaustion	such as having to stop playing netball in the second half
• slowing of reactions/increased reaction time	→	slower to make vital decisions; poorer decisions made	such as goal keeper failing to save a shot on goal
• muscle fatigue	→	causes cramp in muscles	such as being unable to play well towards end of a football match

Worked example

Figure 1 shows a 10 k runner receiving water during the race. Briefly explain why this is important. **(3 marks)**

The 10 k is a long race, therefore water is needed to prevent dehydration due to loss of liquid through sweating, which could lead to muscle cramps, preventing the runner from performing their best.

Figure 1

Remember to use the question to help you. 10 k is a long way, so the performer is likely to get hot and sweat a lot and therefore lose water from the body.

Now try this

1 Give the definition of dehydration. **(1 mark)**
2 State **one** reason why it is important for a games player to remain hydrated. **(1 mark)**

Paper 2 – Extended answer question 1

There will be two extended answer questions at the end of each of your exam papers. One will be a 6-mark question and the other a 9-mark question. To gain all available marks for question 1 you will need to:

- ☑ demonstrate your knowledge and understanding of the topics related to the question
- ☑ apply the topics to relevant situations
- ☑ analyse and evaluate, making judgements about the things you have written.

See pages 115–116 in the Exam skills section for more detail on answering extended answer questions.

Worked example

Ms Harman is planning her after-school basketball practice sessions. One session is with the girls' first team and the other is a session with the new Year 7. She plans to focus on basic passing skills with the new students and free throws with the first team.

Discuss whether Ms Harman would use intrinsic or extrinsic feedback, or a mixture of both, with the two different groups.

(6 marks)

There are several different types of feedback Ms Harman could use: positive or negative; intrinsic or extrinsic; or knowledge of results or knowledge of performance.

With the group of beginners she would use extrinsic feedback; this is feedback from outside the performer. For example, she would tell the girls where to place their hands and where to aim if they did either of these things wrong, as they would not know how to detect and correct their own errors.

Intrinsic feedback is used with those who already have a good grasp of the skill – they know how it should be executed and can feel if they are doing anything wrong, with the ability to correct their own errors. Therefore this type of feedback would be of no use to the beginners. It would, however, be perfect for the first team, as they are experienced and know how to do the skill accurately, and the skill is well learned. If one of the first team was not very good at a particular skill, though, Ms Harman would also use extrinsic feedback with this player, as they would need the additional help so that they understood what they were doing wrong and how to correct it.

Ms Harman would not want to use too much extrinsic feedback with the teams, though, as players can become over-reliant on it and never learn to correct their own errors.

When answering this question you will be assessed on your ability to link ideas together to show your understanding of different topics when applied to sport and physical activity.

Discuss

'Discuss' requires you to give different or contrasting viewpoints, for example, the reasons why you would not use intrinsic feedback with beginners.

For each point you make you should give information about the topic. Here you can see there is general information about types of feedback, and about intrinsic feedback in particular. This knowledge has been applied by linking specific reasons as to why the types of feedback are relevant.

Finally the response should make judgements. In this example reasons are given to support the use of extrinsic feedback with the beginners, and to explain why intrinsic feedback would not work.

Now try this

It is important for any player to control their arousal when playing sport. Discuss the factors that may influence different optimal levels of arousal.

(6 marks)

Paper 2 – Extended answer question 2

There will be two extended answer questions at the end of each of your exam papers. One will be a 6-mark question and the other a 9-mark question. To gain all available marks for question 2 you will need to:

☑ demonstrate your knowledge and understanding of the topics related to the question

☑ apply the topics to relevant situations

☑ evaluate what you have written to justify your answer.

See pages 115–116 in the Exam skills section for more detail on answering extended answer questions.

Worked example

Evaluate why an elite performer might resort to gamesmanship or the use of prohibited substances in their sport. **(9 marks)**

Gamesmanship is bending the rules without actually breaking them.

Prohibited substances in sport are performance-enhancing drugs. They are prohibited because they give the performer an unfair advantage over the other competitors.

An example of gamesmanship is time wasting. For example, in tennis this might be waiting until your opponent is about to serve and then stopping to tie up your shoelace. This is not actually cheating, but it shows poor etiquette, as it can be an effective way to break the rhythm of the server, therefore disrupting their concentration in the hope they go on to serve a double fault.

An example of a performance-enhancing drug in sport is anabolic steroids. A sprinter or other power athlete may take this drug, as it increases their ability to train, increasing their muscle mass so the sprinter can increase their speed. This is cheating and is done to create an unfair advantage, increasing chances of winning.

Performers sometimes resort to both gamesmanship and drug taking because the rewards of winning are so great. For example, the more you win, the better the media exposure you receive. This may mean being selected for higher-paying clubs or increased sponsorship deals.

However, the consequences of cheating are great. Being seen as a drug cheat and having medals or trophies taken away will badly affect the image of the performer, meaning they could lose sponsorship.

> When answering this question you will be assessed on your ability to link ideas together to show your understanding of different topics when applied to sport and physical activity.

Evaluate

'Evaluate' requires a justification, a judgement from available evidence – meaning make your point and build on it to make it clearer. This could be through examples, as shown here, and making a judgement about why people might be deviant in sport.

> Knowledge and understanding of the topic are demonstrated through the points being made. This knowledge is then applied through examples leading to justifications – in this example, why someone might be deviant.

> Use paragraphs to clearly separate your points.

Now try this

Frankie joined a trampoline club. He is just starting to learn how to do back somersaults. Evaluate the type of guidance the coach should use to help Frankie learn this technique. **(9 marks)**

Multiple choice questions

There will be two separate exam papers. You will have 1 hour 15 minutes to complete each exam. Both papers will contain multiple choice, short answer and extended answer questions. There will be several multiple choice questions at the start of both Paper 1 and Paper 2.

Answering multiple choice questions

✓ Highlight the key words in the question.

✓ Read all the options carefully.

✓ Rule out the ones you know are wrong.

✓ Select what you think is the right answer.

✓ Double check the remaining options as well to make sure you are right.

Choosing the best answer

You need to be really careful when you are choosing your answer. There are often choices that look sensible, but aren't suitable for the **context** of the question. Always read the question carefully and choose the **most appropriate** option for the context.

Worked example

Nadine plays football.
Which one of the following fitness tests is most relevant to Nadine's sport?   **(1 mark)**

A Sit and reach test   ○
B Handgrip dynamometer test   ○
C Stork balance   ○
D Illinois agility test   ●

This question is asking you to find the **most** relevant option for the football player. All of the options test components of fitness that would be relevant to a footballer. However, option A tests flexibility, option B tests strength of the lower arm and option C tests static balance, therefore not the **most** relevant to a footballer. In which case, the **most** relevant option for a footballer is option D, as it mimics the action used in a game (dodging between players).

This question is asking you to find the most important component of fitness for the sprinter to get a good start.
You can immediately discount option C, as this is a sprint event. Three options remain. Option B states coordination and, although coordination is required during the race and could impact on the start, it is not as critical for a good start as option A. Option D is strength, and while strength would be important if linked with speed to provide power, this has not been stated. Option A is the best option, as without a good reaction time the sprinter will not get a good start. **Always opt for the most obvious correct response.**

Worked example

Identify which of the following is an essential component of fitness for the sprinter to get a good start.   **(1 mark)**

A Reaction time   ●
B Coordination   ○
C Cardiovascular endurance   ○
D Muscular strength   ○

Short answer questions

Most questions will require you to write short answers. Some of these may only be one-word answers. Others will require a few short sentences or statements. Most short answer questions will be worth 1, 2, 3 or 4 marks.

Answering short answer questions

✓ Read the question carefully.

✓ Highlight or underline key words.

✓ Note the number of marks available for the question.

✓ Make sure you make the same number of statements as there are marks available. For example, if the question is worth 2 marks, make at least 2 statements.

✓ Don't repeat question words. If you do, make sure you go on to explain in further detail using other words too.

✓ If an activity is referred to in the question, make sure your answers relate to this activity.

✓ Give a range of answers rather than all from the same area (unless asked to do so). For example, if asked to give **two** examples, or **two** reasons, make sure they are different and not the same answer phrased in a different way. For example, if you are asked to give **two** reasons for goal setting, you would not gain credit for 'to motivate' and 'to give incentive', as they mean the same thing.

✓ Use the space available in the answer booklet as a guide. The space provided is plenty – be detailed but concise.

Describe vs explain

Different questions have different command words.

✓ If a question asks you to **describe** it is asking for a number of linked statements that give an account of something – you do not need to justify your statements.

✓ However, if you are asked to **explain** make sure you develop your answer, providing justifications for points that you make. You should be using words such as **because** or **therefore** to link statements, leading you to a more in-depth answer.

Worked example

Explain why a high level of cardiovascular endurance is beneficial to a long-distance runner. **(2 marks)**

A high level of cardiovascular endurance is good for long-distance runners **because** they will get more oxygen **transported** to the working muscles. Therefore they can use the oxygen to work aerobically and run at a faster pace for longer and improve their performance.

Worked example

One of the possible mental health benefits of exercise is an increase in self-esteem. Explain how self-esteem can be increased through physical activity. **(2 marks)**

Self-esteem is a form of self-confidence. It can be increased through physical activity because the more you practise a skill, the better you get at it, and being better at something makes you feel good about yourself, which increases your self-esteem.

Note how there are two parts to the answer. The first part explains the term and identifies something that would make you feel better about yourself (improving a skill). The second part gives a reason why this would increase self-esteem.

Use of data questions

You need to be able to demonstrate an understanding of how data is collected, presented and interpreted. Data can be collected based on the quality of what you see, for example how well a skill is performed (qualitative), or based on numbers, such as how many sit-ups are completed (quantitative).

Answering data questions

Some questions will provide you with data and may ask you to analyse it.

Data is just a way of presenting information to make it easier to use.

There is a lot of data in the table showing aerobic endurance levels. This is because different age groups would be expected to achieve different results, as would males and females. You just need to find the result relevant to the question.

Worked example

The table below shows data for different levels of aerobic endurance.
Jayden is 20. He scored 43 in the test.
Identify Jayden's rating for aerobic endurance. **(1 mark)**

Age and gender	Excellent	Good	Fair	Poor
	Maximum oxygen consumption (ml/kg/min)			
15-year-old male	56–52	46–42	41–37	36–32
15-year-old female	53–49	43–39	38–34	33–29
20-year-old male	55–51	45–41	40–36	35–31
20-year-old female	52–48	42–38	37–33	32–28

Interpreting data

Some questions on both exam papers will ask you to interpret and analyse graphical representations of data.

You could be presented with tables, bar charts, line graphs or pie charts.

Golden rule

Use all of the information available.
For example, on a line graph:

✓ look at what the x-axis and the y-axis tell you

✓ then analyse the data by saying what you see.

Remember: the x-axis is the horizontal axis; the y-axis is the vertical one.

Worked example

Using the graph, analyse participation rates in the UK since 2006. **(1 mark)**

Once a week sport participation (millions)

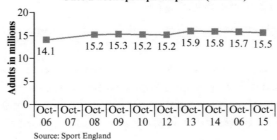

Source: Sport England

There has been a rise in participation since 2006, although numbers have dropped since October 2013.

Presenting data

You may need to present data, using an appropriate type of graph or chart.

- If the information you need to present is continuous, for example showing changes over time (such as recovery heart rate in minutes), you should produce a line graph.

- If the information you need to present is for different categories of data, for example males and females, you should produce a bar graph.

- If you are trying to compare parts of a whole, such as the percentage of carbohydrate in your diet compared to other nutrients, then use a pie chart.

Worked example

Data shows 40.6% of men play sport at least once a week, compared to 30.7% of women.
Complete the graph to show these participation rates. **(2 marks)**

Current differences in sports participaion by gender

Extended answer questions 1

There will be one 6-mark and one 9-mark question on each exam paper. To answer these questions well you need to make sure you demonstrate:

- your knowledge of the topic in the question
- the ability to apply this knowledge and make a reasoned judgement.

For example, if you are asked to evaluate two different types of training, by the end of your response it should be clear which of the types of training you think is best and why.

Tips on answering extended answer questions

- Take time to read the question carefully.
- Look for the key words in the question.
- Underline/highlight those words that tell you what you need to write about.
- Do not just write bullet points.
- Do not simply repeat the question words without explaining them.

Golden rule

It is a very good idea to do a quick plan before you write your extended answer to make sure you cover the key points.

Command words

The command words for the extended answer questions are likely to be one of the following:

- Analyse
- Evaluate
- Discuss
- Justify

All of these words require a judgement as part of the response. Turn to the Command words section on page 124 for more details on the requirements for these words.

When writing your answers to the extended answer questions, you need to plan to demonstrate three things:

1 Your **knowledge**.

2 Your ability to **apply** your knowledge.

3 Your ability to **evaluate** – to make a judgement about the things you have written.

Examples:

1 Naming or describing a type of training demonstrates **knowledge**.

2 Being able to link an appropriate type of training to a specific activity shows **application** of knowledge.

3 Being able to argue why one type of training is better than another for a particular performer demonstrates the ability to **evaluate**.

Key points to remember

For the extended answer questions, unlike other types of question, you do not get a mark for every point you make.

You are marked on your ability to:

- provide a full and balanced answer (which is why it is so important to identify the key words in a question)
- provide an answer that is well written and shows your full understanding of the topic in the question. It is essential that your response relates to all key words.

There is no one correct answer for the extended answer questions.

Extended answer questions can be based on any area of the specification.

The extended answer questions are designed to stretch you. A series of simple statements will not be enough for full marks.

Although you want to demonstrate knowledge application and your ability to evaluate, even if you can't do all of these things, make sure you **attempt** the question as any relevant content about the topic **will** gain some credit.

Extended answer questions 2

Here is an example of an extended answer question, a possible answer and some notes to guide you.

Worked example

Penny is a 100 m sprinter and runs for the county. Her friend Kam plays tennis for the county. Both need to work on their fitness for their sport.
With reference to the musculo-skeletal system, evaluate whether Penny and Kam should use weight training to improve their performance. **(9 marks)**

> The question asks you to **evaluate** therefore you need to make a decision based on whether you think Penny and Kam should use weight training. This decision should be based on the rest of your answer. Just saying 'yes' or 'no' will not gain credit!

> Mentioning the benefits of weight training is a good way to start, as it shows your **knowledge** of the impact of the training method on one of the systems mentioned in the question.

> Don't forget to demonstrate your knowledge across all aspects of the question; this means you need to talk about the skeletal system too. This part of the answer starts with **knowledge** then goes on to **application** of knowledge.

Weight training will increase both performers' muscular strength. The muscles will adapt and increase in size. Strength is a component of power. With an increase in strength it is possible to generate greater power, and this would be good for both performers. If Penny had more power she could apply more force to the track and therefore run faster in her event.

The skeletal system would become denser as a result of weight training, and the strength of bones and ligaments would increase, improving joint stability. There would also be increased production of synovial fluid and overall flexibility.

> By linking the adaptations from the training methods to the performers in the question, you are **applying** your knowledge.

These adaptations would benefit both performers. For example, Kam would be less likely to dislocate her shoulder when striking the ball, and Penny would be less likely to suffer a hairline fracture during training, allowing her to continue to train and preventing reversibility.

If Kam increased her power she would be able to hit the ball harder so that her shots, for example her serve, would be harder to return.

One problem with an increase in muscle size is that the body becomes heavier (owing to the extra muscle), meaning more energy is required to move the additional weight. This could have a negative effect on Kam, because if she becomes too muscular it will take more energy to move around the court and she will need to conserve her energy to last the whole match. Kam would be less reliant on power than Penny, as other factors are important in her game such as cardiovascular fitness and the skill to play the different shots. Therefore while Kam may do weight training, she would not wish to gain as much power as Penny.

Overall, weight training would provide benefits for both performers and therefore could be added to their training schedule. However, it would not meet all of the performers' needs, therefore other training methods should also be included and in fact weight training should only be done in moderation for Kam.

> Once you have made some points you can use these to support any **judgement** you make. For example, by identifying what is good about weight training for the performers, you are supporting the judgement that they should use this training method.

Preparing for your exam

Checklist for exam day
- ☑ Eat well
- ☑ Get there early

Remember:
- ☑ Pens (yes, more than one; they always run out on exam day!)
- ☑ Pencil – for drawing diagrams or graphs
- ☑ Ruler
- ☑ Eraser
- ☑ Write neatly
- ☑ Spell as well as you can. If in doubt, sound it out and spell the word as it sounds

Go for your own personal gold!
Preparing for your PE exam is the same as preparing for any event. So train for it!

Practice
The more you practise (revise), the more you will understand. The more you train, the better your performance.

Pace yourself
You need to peak at the right time, so plan your revision. You can still do other things if you are organised. Put the topics in your diary and stick to the plan.

Don't stay up late the night before your exam: you want to be at your best for your 'event'.

Good luck and see you on the podium!

Subject-specific vocabulary

You should understand these terms and their use.

Ability: Inherited, stable traits that determine an individual's potential to learn or acquire a skill.

Adaptability: The potential to change with ease.

Adrenaline: Natural hormone released to speed heart rate up.

Aerobic: With oxygen. When exercise is not too fast and is steady, the heart can supply all the oxygen that the working muscles need.
Summarised as: glucose + oxygen → energy + carbon dioxide + water.

Aerobic training zone: The aerobic training zone allows the aerobic system to be trained. To define aerobic training zone:
1. Calculate maximum heart rate (220bpm) minus age: 220 – age.
2. Work at 60–80% of maximum heart rate.

Aggression: A deliberate intent to harm or injure another person, which can be physical or mental (see direct and indirect aggression).

Agility: The ability to move and change direction quickly (at speed) while maintaining control.

Agonist (prime mover): Muscle or group responsible for the movement.

Altitude: A geographical area (of land) which is over 2000 m above sea level.

Altitude sickness: Nausea caused by training at altitude.

Alveoli: Air sacs in the lungs.

Amateur: This term defines someone who:
- takes part in an activity as a hobby, rather than for financial gain
- has another main job outside of sport
- takes part for fun
- could be at a lower level.

Anabolic steroids: Artificially produced male hormones mimicking testosterone. They promote muscle and bone growth, and reduce recovery time. Often used by power athletes, such as sprinters.

Anaerobic: Without oxygen. When exercise duration is short and at high intensity, the heart and lungs cannot supply blood and oxygen to muscles as fast as the respiring cells need them.
Summarised as: glucose → energy + lactic acid.

Antagonist: Acts to produce the opposite action to the agonist. They work in antagonistic pairs.

Arousal: A physical and mental (physiological and psychological) state of alertness/readiness, varying from deep sleep to intense excitement/alertness.

Articulating bones: Where two or more bones meet to allow movement at a joint.

Axis: Imaginary line through the body around which it rotates. Types of axis:
- longitudinal (or vertical): head to toe
- transverse: through the hips
- sagittal: through the belly button.

Backflow: The flowing backwards of blood. Valves in the veins prevent this from happening.

Balance: The maintenance of the centre of mass over the base of support. Reference can be made to static (while still) or dynamic (while moving).

Balanced diet: It is defined as eating:
- the right amount (for energy expended)
- the right amount of calories
- according to how much you exercise
- different food types to provide suitable nutrients, vitamins and minerals.

Beta blockers: Drugs that are used to steady nerves by controlling heart rate. They have a calming and relaxing effect.

Blood doping: Defined by World Anti-Doping Agency (WADA) as the misuse of techniques and/ or substances to increase one's red blood cell count.

Blood pressure: The pressure that blood is under. Types of pressure:
- systolic: when the heart is contracting
- diastolic: when the heart is relaxed.

Body composition: The percentage of body weight that is fat and non-fat (muscle and bone).

Calorie: A unit that measures heat or energy production in the body, normally expressed as Kcal.

Carbohydrate: The body's preferred energy source.

Cardiac cycle: The process of the heart going through the stages of systole and diastole (see Blood pressure) in the atria and ventricles (see Heart chambers).

Cardiac output: The amount of blood ejected from the heart in one minute or: stroke volume × heart rate.

Cardiovascular endurance (aerobic power): The ability of the heart and lungs to supply oxygen to the working muscles.

Circuit training: A series of exercise stations whereby periods of work are interspersed with periods of rest.

Closed season: Post (transition). It is defined as:
- period of rest to recuperate
- players doing gentle aerobic exercise to maintain general fitness
- being fully rested and ready for pre-season training.

Closed skill: A skill that is not affected by the environment or performers within it. The skill tends to be done the same way each time.

Commercialisation: To manage or exploit (an organisation, activity, etc.) in a way designed to make a profit. The specification refers to commercialised activity as being sponsorship and the media only.

Competition season (peak): It is defined as:
- playing season
- taking part in matches every week
- maintenance of fitness related to the activity but not too much training as it may cause fatigue, which would decrease performance
- concentration on skills/set plays to improve team performance.

Continuous training: Involves working for a sustained period of time without rest. It improves cardiovascular fitness. Sometimes referred to as a steady state training.

Contract to compete: Unwritten agreement to follow and abide by the written and unwritten rules.

Coordination: The ability to use different (two or more) parts of the body together, smoothly and efficiently.

Deep breathing: Slow, deep breaths while relaxed.

Dehydration: Excessive loss of body water, interrupting the function of the body.

Delayed onset of muscle soreness (DOMS): The pain felt in the muscles the day after exercise.

Direct aggression: Aggressive act that involves physical contact with others, such as a punch.

Diuretics: Drugs that remove fluid from the body, elevating the rate of bodily urine excretion.

Ectomorph: A somatotype characterised by being tall and thin. Individuals with narrow shoulders and narrow hips.

Embolism: Blockage of a blood vessel.

Endomorph: A somatotype, characterised by a pear shaped body/fatness. Individuals with wide hips and narrow shoulders.

Erythropoietin (EPO): A type of peptide hormone that increases the red blood cell count.

Etiquette: A convention or unwritten rule in an activity. It is not an enforceable rule but it is usually observed.

Excess post-exercise oxygen consumption (EPOC): Sometimes referred to as oxygen debt (now an outdated term), EPOC refers to the amount of oxygen needed to recover after exercise. EPOC enables lactic acid to be converted to glucose, carbon dioxide and water (using oxygen). It explains why we continue to breathe deeply and quickly after exercise.

Expiration: Breathing out.

Externally paced skill: A skill that is started because of an external factor. The speed, rate or pace of the skill is controlled by external factors, such as an opponent.

Extrinsic feedback: Received from outside of the performer, such as from a coach. See Intrinsic feedback for a comparison.

Extrovert: Sociable, active, talkative, outgoing personality type usually associated with team sports players.

Fartlek training: Swedish for 'speed play'. Periods of fast work with intermittent periods of slower work. Often used in running, for example: sprint, jog, walk, jog, sprint.

Fatigue: Either physical or mental, fatigue is a feeling of extreme or severe tiredness due to a build-up of lactic acid or working for long periods of time.

Feedback: Information a performer receives about their performance. Feedback can be given during and/or after performance.

Fine movement (skill classification): Small and precise movement, showing high levels of accuracy and coordination. It involves the use of a small group of muscles.

Fitness: The ability to meet/cope with the demands of the environment.

FITT principle: FITT is used to increase the amount of work the body does, in order to achieve overload (see SPORT). FITT stands for:
- frequency: how often you train
- intensity: how hard you train
- time: the length of the training session
- type: the specific method, such as continuous training.

Flexibility: The range of movements possible at a joint.

Gamesmanship: Attempting to gain an advantage by stretching the rules to their limit, for example time wasting.

Gross movement (skill classification): Using large muscle groups to perform big, strong, powerful movements.

Guidance: A method to convey information to a performer. Guidance methods:
- visual (seeing)
- verbal (hearing)
- manual (assist movement – physical)
- mechanical (use of objects/aids).

Haemoglobin: The substance in the red blood cells that transports oxygen (as oxyhaemoglobin) and carbon dioxide.

Health: A state of complete physical, mental and social well-being, and not merely the absence of disease or infirmity (as per the World Health Organization, WHO). Ill health refers to being in a state of poor physical, mental and/or social well-being.

Heart attack: It occurs when the flow of oxygen-rich blood to a section of heart muscle suddenly becomes blocked.

Heart chambers: They include the right and left atria and ventricles.

Heart rate: The number of times the heart beats (usually measured per minute).

High altitude training (traditional): Training at altitude (2000 m above sea level or higher) where there is less oxygen. The body adapts by making more red blood cells to carry oxygen. The additional oxygen carrying red blood cells is an advantage for endurance athletes returning to sea level to compete.

High intensity interval training (HIIT): An exercise strategy alternating periods of short, intense anaerobic exercise with less intense recovery periods (see Interval training).

Home-field advantage: Gaining an advantage in a sporting event from being in familiar surroundings, with the majority of the spectators supporting you.

Hooliganism: Disorderly, aggressive and often violent behaviour by spectators at sporting events.

Hydration: Having enough water to enable normal functioning of the body.

Hypertension: High blood pressure in the arteries.

Hypertrophy: The enlargement of an organ or tissue from the increase in the size of its cells.

Indirect aggression: Aggression that does not involve physical contact. The aggression is taken out on an object to gain advantage, such as hitting a tennis ball hard during a rally.

Information processing: Making decisions. Gathering data from the display (senses), prioritising the most important stimuli to make a suitable decision.

Inspiration: Breathing in.

Interval training: Periods of training/work that are followed by periods of rest, for example work, rest, work, rest (see High intensity interval training).

Intrinsic feedback: It's a type of intrinsic feedback, received via receptors in the muscles. These are sensations that are felt by the performer, providing information from movement.

Introvert: A quiet, passive, reserved, shy personality type, usually associated with individual sports performance.

Isometric contraction: Muscle contraction where the length of the muscle does not alter. The contraction is constant, so pushing against a load.

Isotonic contraction: Muscle contraction that results in limb movement:
- concentric contraction – shortening of the muscle
- eccentric contraction – lengthening of the muscle.

Level playing field: The same for all competitors.

Lever: A rigid bar (bone) that turns about an axis to create movement. The force to move the lever comes from the muscle(s). Each lever contains:
- a fulcrum – fixed point, effort (from the muscle(s) to move it)
- load/resistance (from gravity).

Lifestyle: See Sedentary lifestyle.

Masculinity: Displaying masculine (male) stereotypical behaviour.

Maximum heart rate: Calculated by: 220 – age.

Mechanical advantage: The efficiency of a working lever, calculated by: effort ÷ weight (resistance) arm.

Media: Diversified technologies that act as the main means of mass communication. These include:
- printed media (such as newspapers)
- broadcast media (such as TV and radio)
- internet/social media (such as Facebook)
- outdoor media (such as billboards).

Mental health and well-being: A state of well-being in which every individual realises his/her own potential, can cope with the normal stresses of life, can work productively and fruitfully, and is able to make a contribution to her or his community (as per WHO). It works in conjunction with physical and social health.

Mental rehearsal/visualisation/imagery: Cognitive relaxation techniques involving control of mental thoughts and imagining positive outcomes.

Mesomorph: A somatotype, characterised by a muscular appearance. Individuals with wide shoulders and narrow hips.

Minerals: Inorganic substances that assist the body with many of its functions, such as bone formation (calcium).

Motivation (intrinsic motivation and extrinsic motivation): The drive to succeed or the desire (want) to achieve something/to be inspired to do something. This can be:
- intrinsic – the drive that comes from within (for pride, satisfaction, a sense of accomplishment, self-worth)
- extrinsic – the drive to perform well or to win in order to gain external rewards (such as prizes, money, praise).

Movement at a joint: Classified into:
- flexion – decrease in the angle of the bones at a joint
- extension: increasing the angle of bones at a joint
- abduction: movement away from the midline of the body
- adduction: movement towards the midline of the body
- rotation: movement around an axis
- plantar flexion: pointing the toes at the ankle/ increasing the ankle angle
- dorsiflexion: flexing toes up at the ankle/ decreasing the ankle angle.

Muscular endurance (similar to dynamic strength): Ability of a muscle or muscle group to undergo repeated contractions, avoiding fatigue.

Narcotic analgesics: Drugs that can be used to reduce the feeling of pain.

Nutrition: The intake of food, considered in relation to the body's dietary needs. Good nutrition is an adequate, well-balanced diet, combined with regular physical activity.

Obese: A term used to describe people with a large fat content, caused by an imbalance of calories consumed to energy expenditure. A body mass index (BMI) of over 30 or over 20% above standard weight for height ratio.

One rep max: The maximal amount that can be lifted in one repetition by a muscle/group of muscles (with the correct technique).

Open skill: A skill that is performed in a certain way to deal with a changing or unstable environment, such as to outwit an opponent.

Outcome goals: Focus on end result/winning.

Peptide hormones: Drugs that stimulate the production of naturally occurring hormones (for example, EPO), which increase red blood cell count/oxygen-carrying capacity.

Performance goals: Personal standards to be achieved. Performers compare themselves against what they have already done or suggest what they are going to do. There is no comparison with other performers.

Physical health and well-being: All body systems working well, free from illness and injury. Ability to carry out everyday tasks. It works in conjunction with social and mental health.

Physiology: Study of how our cells, muscles and organs work together, and how they interact.

Plane: Imaginary lines depicting the direction of movement. Types of planes:
- sagittal: forwards and backwards
- frontal: left or right
- transverse: rotation around the longitudinal axis.

Positive self-talk: Developing cognitive positive thoughts about your own performance.

Post-season (transition): Period of rest/active recovery/light aerobic work after the competition period (season).

Power/explosive strength (anaerobic power): The product of strength and speed, or: strength × speed.

Pre-season (preparation): It is defined as:
- period leading up to competition
- usually using continuous/fartlek/interval training sessions to increase aerobic fitness
- weight training to build up strength and muscular endurance
- developing techniques specific to the sport in order to be fully prepared for matches at start of season and therefore be more successful.

Prime mover (agonist): Muscle or muscle group responsible for the movement.

Principles of overload: Frequency, intensity, time and type (see FITT).

Principles of training: Specificity, progressive overload, reversibility and tedium (see SPORT).

Pulse raiser: Any activity that raises heart rate. Usually as part of a warm up, such as a light jog.

Qualitative: More of a subjective than an objective appraisal. Involving opinions relating to the quality of a performance rather than the quantity (such as score, placing, number).

Quantitative: A measurement that can be quantified as a number, such as time in seconds or goals scored. There is no opinion expressed (qualitative). It is a fact.

Reaction time: The time taken to initiate a response to a stimulus, for example the time from the initiation of the stimulus (such as the starting gun in 100 m) to starting to initiate a response (starting to move out of the blocks in 100 m).

Recovery: Time required to repair the damage to the body caused by training or competition.

Rehydration: Consuming water to restore hydration.

Reliability: Relating to the consistency and repeatability of a test (to produce the same or similar scores, for example).

Repetitions: The number of times an individual action is performed. A set is a group of repetitions.

Residual volume: Volume of air left in the lungs after maximal expiration.

Role model: A person looked to by others as an example to be imitated.

Season: A period of time during which competition takes place or training seasons, dividing the year up into sectional parts for pre-determined benefits. Training seasons include:
- pre-season (preparation)
- competition season (peak)
- post-season (transition).
  See these terms for definitions.

Sedentary lifestyle: A lifestyle with irregular or no physical activity.

Self-paced skill: The skill is started when the performer decides to start it. The speed, rate or pace of the skill is controlled by the performer.

Skeletal system: Skeletal system provides a framework of bones for movement, in conjunction with the muscular system.

Skill: A learned action/learned behaviour with the intention of bringing about pre-determined results, with maximum certainty and minimum outlay of time and energy.

Skill classification: Categorisation of sporting skills in accordance with set continua. These include:
- simple/complex continua
- open/closed continua
- self-paced/externally paced continua
- gross/fine continua.

SMART targets: For goals to be successful they must be SMART:
- specific: specific to the demands of the sport/muscles used/movements used
- measurable: it must be possible to measure whether they have been met
- accepted: they must be accepted by the performer and others involved, for example a coach
- realistic: they are actually possible to complete
- time bound: over a set period of time.

Social health and well-being: Basic human needs are being met (food, shelter and clothing). The individual has friendship and support, some value in society, is socially active and has little stress in social circumstances. It works in conjunction with physical and mental health.

Somatotype: A method of classifying body type. Body types:
- ectomorph
- endomorph
- mesomorph.
See these terms for definitions of individual somatotypes.

Speed: The maximum rate at which an individual is able to perform a movement or cover a distance in a period of time, putting the body parts into action as quickly as possible. Calculated by: distance ÷ time.

Spirometer trace: A measure of lung volumes, which includes:
- tidal volume: volume of air inspired or expired/exchanged per breath
- inspiratory reserve volume: the amount of air that could be breathed in after tidal volume
- expiratory reserve volume: the amount of air that could be breathed out after tidal volume
- residual volume: the amount of air left in the lungs after maximal expiration.

Sponsor: An individual or group that provides financial support to an event, activity, person or organisation.

Sponsorship: Provision of funds or other forms of support to an individual or event in return for some commercial return.

SPORT (the principles of training)

- **Specificity:** Making training specific to the sport being played/movements used/muscles used/energy system(s) used.
- **Progressive overload:** Gradual increase of the amount of overload so that fitness gains occur, but without potential for injury. Overload is the gradual increase of stress placed upon the body during exercise training (more than normal).
- **Reversibility:** Losing fitness levels when you stop exercising.
- **Tedium:** Boredom that can occur from training the same way every time. Variety is needed.

Sportsmanship: Conforming to the rules, spirit and etiquette of a sport.

Static stretching: Holding a stretch still/held/isometric.

Stimulants: Drugs that have an effect on the central nervous system, for example by increasing mental and/or physical alertness.

Strength: The ability to overcome a resistance. This can be explosive, static or dynamic:
- explosive: see Power
- static: static ability to hold a body part (limb) in a static position. Muscle length stays the same maximum force that can be applied to an immoveable object
- dynamic: see Muscular endurance for similarity.

Stroke volume: The volume of blood pumped out of the heart by each ventricle during one contraction.

Submaximal: Working below maximal intensity level.

Suppleness: As with flexibility, the range of movement possible at a joint.

Synovial joint: An area of the body where two or more bones meet (articulate) to allow a range of movements. The ends of the bones are covered in articular cartilage and are enclosed in a capsule filled with fluid. For the purposes of this specification, the following structural features and roles should be known:
- synovial membrane: secretes synovial fluid
- synovial fluid: provides lubrication
- joint capsule: encloses/supports
- bursae (sacks of fluid): reduce friction
- cartilage – prevents friction/bones rubbing together
- ligaments: attach bone to bone.

Tangible: Something that can be seen and touched, such as a trophy.

Target zone: The range within which athletes need to work for aerobic training to take place (60–80% of maximum heart rate).

Training: A well-planned programme that uses scientific principles to improve performance, skill, game ability, motor and physical fitness.

Training thresholds: The actual boundaries of the target zone.

Validity: The extent to which a test or method measures what it sets out to measure.

Viscosity: Thickening of the blood.

Vitamins: Organic substances that are required for many essential processes in the body, such as Vitamin A for structure and function of the skin.

Weight training: The use of weights/resistance to cause adaptation of the muscles.

Well-being: Involves physical, mental and social well-being. The dynamic process that gives people a sense of being comfortable, healthy or happy.

Command words

Command words are the words used in assessment tasks that tell you how you should answer the question.

Analyse: Separate information into components and identify their characteristics.

Apply: Put into effect in a recognised way.

Calculate: Work out the value of something.

Compare: Identify similarities and/or differences.

Complete: Finish a task by adding to given information.

Consider: Review and respond to given information.

Define: Specify meaning.

Describe: Set out characteristics.

Discuss: Present key points about different ideas or strengths and weaknesses of an idea.

Evaluate: Judge from available evidence.

Explain: Set out purposes or reasons.

Identify: Name or otherwise characterise.

Illustrate: Present clarifying examples.

Interpret: Translate information into recognisable form.

Justify: Support a case with evidence.

Outline: Set out main characteristics.

Suggest: Present a possible case/solution.

State: Express clearly and briefly.

Answers

The following pages contain examples of answers that could be made to the 'Now try this' questions throughout the Revision Guide. In many cases these are not the only correct answers.

Applied anatomy and physiology

1. Bones of the skeleton
femur (1); tibia (1)

2. Structure of the skeleton
The cranium is an example of a flat bone (1). The bone covers the brain therefore provides protection (1), absorbing the impact of the ball hitting the head so that the brain is not damaged when the player heads the ball (1).

3. Functions of the skeleton
The skeleton aids movement by providing a place for the muscles to attach to (1). This means when the muscles contract they pull on the bones to create movement (1).

4. Structure of a synovial joint
Bursae cushion impact within the joint (1), therefore, when the player is thrown there is less chance of damage to the joint (1), so the performer can continue to train and compete (1).

5. Types of freely moveable joints
A: Ball and socket (1)

6. Movement at joints 1
Flexion of the arm at the elbow (1)

7. Movement at joints 2
Abduction to adduction (1)

8. Movement at joints 3
Plantar flexion is occurring at the ankle (1). This will allow the volleyball player to use her toes to push off from the floor to gain greater height (1).

9. Muscles
Shoulder abduction (1). An example is the preparation phase of an overarm throw in cricket (1).

10. Antagonistic pairs: biceps and triceps
triceps (1); biceps (1)

11. Antagonistic pairs: quadriceps and hamstrings
Quadriceps (1)

12. Antagonistic pairs: gastrocnemius and tibialis anterior
Tibialis anterior (1)

13. Antagonistic pairs: hip flexors and gluteals
Hip flexors (1); hip flexion (1)

14. Muscle contractions
Eccentric muscle contraction is when the muscle lengthens during the contraction (1), whereas concentric muscle contraction is where the muscle shortens as it contracts (1). For example, in the downwards phase of a squat, the quadriceps lengthen but are still working to control the downwards movement (1).

15. The pathway of air
After passing through the trachea, the air travels into the bronchi (1) then into the lungs (1) and then bronchioles (1) before reaching the alveoli (1).

16. Gaseous exchange
(a) high concentration (1)
(b) The blood in the capillaries has just exchanged gases at the alveoli, so has collected oxygen to take to the muscles. (1)

17. Blood vessels
arteries (1)

18. Redistribution of blood
redistribution of blood (1); increased blood flow (1)

19. Heart structure and the cardiac cycle
right atrium (1); valve (1)

20. Cardiac output
(a) Student C (1)
(b) Student A (1)
(c) Student C (1)

21. Mechanics of breathing
External intercostals (1); diaphragm (1); sternocleidomastoid (1)

22. Lung volumes
(a) The lines on the graph become much larger when Michael is working maximally, as these represent inspiratory and expiratory reserve volumes (1), which Michael will need to use to increase his depth of breathing (1).
The graph shows Michael recovering immediately after the last highest point, as the volume of air reduces but does not go back to the starting volumes (1), because breathing will still be elevated to help with recovery (1).
(b) The trace should show an increase in depth of breathing again (1).

23. Aerobic and anaerobic exercise
(a) Tennis matches can last hours, so when playing for this length of time tennis can be considered aerobic exercise (1).

(b) However, tennis can also be anaerobic exercise, for example when serving the ball as hard as possible (1).

24. Excess post-exercise oxygen consumption (EPOC)

EPOC occurs after exercise during recovery (1), to get additional oxygen into the body compared to what would usually be consumed at rest (1), to break down the build-up of lactic acid (1) that happens when the performer works anaerobically (1).

25. Recovery from exercise

The triathlete will use a lot of carbohydrate to complete his race (1), therefore his carbohydrate needs to be replaced otherwise he will not have enough energy to compete again (1). The 100 m is a much shorter race and more intense, so a 100 m sprinter would not use the same level of carbohydrate as a triathlete (1). A 100 m sprinter is therefore less in need of carbohydrate after activity (1).

26. Effects of exercise 1

Increased frequency of breathing means more breaths of air are taken into the lungs, so more oxygen can be diffused into the blood stream (1) and more carbon dioxide can be exhaled (1). This is an advantage to a games player, as more oxygen will be available for energy for the total length of the game (1).

27. Effects of exercise 2

The muscular system is affected by becoming stronger (1), which benefits the performer; for example, in tennis they would be able to hit the ball with more force (1).

Movement analysis

28. Lever systems 1

(a) The rower is using a first class lever. (1)
(b) It is a first class lever because the fulcrum is between the load and the effort. (1)

29. Lever systems 2

This is a second class lever (1). This means there will be a long effort arm compared to the resistance arm (1). Therefore, a relatively small amount of effort is needed by the sprinter's muscles to move her weight and allow her to accelerate (1).

30. Planes and axes of movement 1

The transverse axis goes from side to side (1); movement will occur in the sagittal plane (1).

31. Planes and axes of movement 2

Movement occurs in the sagittal plane (1) about the transverse axis (1).

Physical training

32. The relationship between health and fitness

Provided you exercise sensibly, in other words have appropriate rest times between sessions, regular exercise can bring a number of health benefits (1). These benefits could be physical, social or mental (1). For example, an increase in fitness due to regular aerobic training can reduce the risk of heart disease (1).

33. Agility

The cricket player would be able to turn quickly at the end of their first run (1), so that they can get a second run, thereby reducing the chance of being run out between wickets as they have spent less time 'turning' (1).

34. Balance and coordination

When a golfer is taking a putt, they use their hand (holding the club) and eyes together (1) to allow them to hit the ball accurately into the hole (1).

Meanwhile, a swimmer during a 100 m butterfly race must coordinate movement of arms and legs at the same time (1) to ensure an efficient stroke, allowing greater generation of power (1).

35. Cardiovascular endurance

Jo and Jus will need to play for 80 minutes without tiring (1) if they are to maintain the quality of their performance throughout the game (1).

36. Flexibility

Flexibility will help Sue and Jenny increase their range of movement at the shoulder joint, allowing them to stretch further (1); for example, for a rebound if the basket is missed (1).

37. Muscular endurance

Muscular endurance is the ability of a muscle or muscle group to undergo repeated contractions, avoiding fatigue (1). Ashley will use the muscular endurance in his arms (1) to keep working his arm muscles as he rows, allowing him to row 3 km without needing to stop and rest (1).

38. Power and speed

Who	Power used to:	Impact
Sprinter	(i) To apply a greater force against the starting blocks (1)	An explosive start
Basketball player	(ii) To get greater height for the jump (1)	Close to hoop to score
(iii) Tennis player serving (1)	(iv) To hit the ball very hard (1)	(v) Harder to return the ball so they can win the point (1)

39. Reaction time

If the ball clips the top of the net, it could be deflected (1), therefore the tennis player needs to respond quickly to this new stimulus by making a fast decision to change their direction (1), so they can get to the ball in time before it hits the floor (1).

40. Strength

The gymnast needs static strength to be able to hold his own body weight in the position (1).

41. Fitness testing

Example answer: \To identify the performers' strengths (1); to monitor any improvement in fitness (1); to motivate (1)

42. Agility and speed tests

The Illinois agility test mimics the dodging movement in a game when swerving in and out of the cones (1), therefore it measures the skill of agility, which is required in a football game to keep possession of the ball (1). Although strength and flexibility are important to a footballer, they are not as important within the game, as it is possible to play well without high levels of grip strength or flexibility (1).

43. Coordination and reaction time tests

The ruler drop test is a test of reaction time (1). The person taking the test would stand with their hand ready to catch the ruler, the 0 m mark between their thumb and forefinger (1). When the ruler is dropped they catch it as soon as possible and the distance from 0 cm is measured (1).

44. Cardiovascular endurance and balance tests

Example answer:
Equipment 1: cones (1); to mark the 20 m distance the runner has to run between on each bleep (1).
Equipment 2: audio equipment (1); to play the bleeps that set the time within which the runners have to complete each 20 m shuttle (1).

45. Strength and flexibility tests

First, the information would be used to identify Liam's rating, which is below average (1). The coach would use this as baseline data (1), so that when Liam is retested after training he could see whether his flexibility had improved (1).

46. Power and muscular endurance tests

Rowers use repeated contractions of the muscles in their trunk when rowing (1), and the sit-up bleep test repeatedly uses the muscles in the trunk, so would reflect the activity (1).

47. Fitness testing: data collection

It is important to analyse and evaluate fitness test results to be able to identify strengths and weaknesses (1) and design appropriate training programmes (1).

48. Principles of training 1

The exercise bike is most likely to be used (1), as it most closely matches the required actions of the sport (1), as when cycling on the bike the cyclist is training the same muscles they will use in their event (1).

49. Principles of training 2

Elad should measure how long he can run without a break, then increase this amount slightly in the next session (1). For example, he could run for 20 minutes at the same pace, then try extending this to 25 minutes (1). He could then continue to increase the time gradually as his body gets used to the new workload, so his cardiovascular endurance continues to improve (1).

50. Principles of training 3

Option D – How long, hard and often you work, making sure that your training fits the requirements of the activity (1)

51. Circuit training

Different exercises are organised at stations (1); performers work on each station for a set period of time before moving on to the next station (1); can be fitness-based or skill-based (1).

52. Continuous training

Continuous training develops cardiovascular endurance and muscular endurance (1), both of which are required in long-distance running (1).

53. Fartlek training

You should include sprinting to mirror what you need to do in a game: for example, sprint 20 m to mimic losing a marker and sprinting for a free ball in a game (1). You should include jogging to mirror moments of recovery in a game after a period of high intensity, such as when you jog back into position (1).

54. Interval training

breaks are built into the session (1); the breaks allow recovery (1); the session is made up of sets of reps of work periods and rest periods (1)

55. Static stretching

The partner can gently apply a force to help you stretch further than you could on your own (1).

56. Weight training

To increase muscular strength, you need fewer repetitions but greater resistance or heavier weights (1). To increase muscular endurance rather than muscular strength, you increase the number of repetitions and reduce the weight lifted, so your muscles get used to working for longer periods of time (1).

57. Plyometric training

Volleyball players need to jump high (1); plyometrics would develop the power in their legs (1), so they would be able to block the ball more easily at the net (1).

58. Training types: pros and cons

If something is boring, then motivation can be lost (1). This may result in the performer stopping training (1) and their performance/fitness levels then dropping (1).

59. Training intensities

line B (1)

60. Injury prevention

1 Performers can make sure they wear appropriate clothing (1), for example, shin pads in hockey (1).
2 They can apply taping to support the joint and to help prevent an injury (1). For example, taping the ankle supports the ankle ligaments, reducing the risk of a sprained ankle during the game (1).

61. High altitude training

1 The performer may need to reduce training intensity at the start of altitude training (1), owing to the lack of oxygen at altitude (1).
2 The performer will need to spend a few weeks at altitude for the training to be effective (1), as the adaptations to the body take time (1).

62. Seasonal training

Pre-season (1); competition (1); post-season (1)

63. Warm up

B: The warm up decreases the amount of lactic acid present and therefore reduces the likelihood of muscle soreness after the activity has finished (1)

64. Cool down

after (1), two (1), jogging (1), stretching (1), soreness (1), flexibility (1)

Paper 1 Extended answer questions

Marks are awarded for the depth and breadth of knowledge demonstrated about the question topics, the application of this knowledge to the context of the question, and the level of evaluation made. The use of appropriate essay format and correct terminology in a structured and coherent way is also taken in to consideration when awarding credit.

65. Paper 1 – Extended answer question 1

Example answer:

Vasoconstriction and vasodilation of the blood vessels allows the redistribution of blood flow within the body. This means that the body is able to increase blood flow to some areas and decrease it to others. For example, at the start of the football match, through vasoconstriction, blood flow is diverted away from the digestive system and through vasodilation it is directed instead to the active muscles. This is because not so much blood is required for digestion and can be sent to areas where the need is greater, to help with performance.

An increased blood flow to the working muscles means that they will receive more oxygenated blood, as oxygen is transported in the blood. With more oxygen, the player will be able to maintain the standard of their play for the duration of the match, for example, continuing to perform effective tackles even late on in the game.

However, there is a drawback: the performer would not be able to eat just before they played or at half-time if they were feeling hungry. This could leave them with low energy levels for the second half; therefore they may need to eat a sports bar or something similar that is easy to digest.

Despite the potential problem with not being able to eat, the advantage of the extra oxygen clearly outweighs the chance that someone is hungry, as they can always make sure they get enough to eat on match days in plenty of time before they play.

Also, although the player will not be running all of the time in the game, they still need an elevated supply of oxygen and therefore blood flow as they will need to recover in between bouts of high-intensity exercise. For example, after chasing a loose ball and passing it on they will need to walk or jog back to position, ready for the next high-intensity demand. Therefore, they will need to be able to regulate blood flow to allow for this as well. Without the ability to recover quickly, they would soon stop being effective in the game; for example, they would not be able to run on to through balls or fast breaks.

66. Paper 1 – Extended answer question 2

Example answer:

Injury prevention methods are designed to reduce risk. These methods include wearing appropriate clothing. For example, a boxer will wear gloves on his hands to protect them from bruising or breaking when he strikes his opponent. Without these gloves the boxer would damage his hands, making them too painful to continue to exert force against his opponent, therefore he would have to give up the fight. Similarly, in badminton appropriate footwear should be worn to reduce the risk of the player slipping when moving on the court and overstretching, as pulling a muscle would result in them having to drop out of the match. Both athletes should also warm up before their main activity, as, if they failed to warm up, they would be more likely to pull a muscle, or be less prepared mentally for the activity, which might mean losing a few early points in badminton, or a knockout in boxing if they are not ready for their opponent.

During their activities both athletes should make sure they drink enough water. It is important they remain hydrated if the quality of their performance is to be maintained.

Finally, both performers should make sure they have a long enough rest period after their activity before doing it again, so their bodies have the chance to recover from the exercise session. If they fail to do this they could overtrain, causing significant injury, which could put them out of action for some time. For example, if either performer does a lot of road running they could get shin splints and would need time to allow this to recover.

Despite the more obvious risk in boxing, if either athlete fails to adequately protect themselves against the risks that exist in their activities, they are likely to suffer an injury and therefore be prevented from playing, leading to loss of fitness and reversibility.

Sports psychology

67. Classification of skills 1
An open skill is one that is affected by the environment (1).

68. Classification of skills 2
(a) complex (1); (b) more basic than (a) (1)

69. Types of goal
They focus on the end result (1), so if you don't win you don't achieve the goal, which can be demotivating (1).

70. Goal setting 1
Targets should be measurable so you can see whether you have achieved them (1).

71. Goal setting 2
realistic (1)

72. Information processing
The long-term memory is used to store information (1) for future use (1), whereas the short-term memory only holds information for a few seconds (1), just for the time you need to execute a skill (1).

73. Visual and verbal guidance
visual guidance (1); beginners (1)

74. Manual and mechanical guidance
C: Performers are supported completing the skill (1)

75. Types of feedback
Overall the performer is getting better as they go from 1 to 7 on the success scale (1). It is possible that no feedback is given for the first three attempts, but the increase on the fourth and fifth attempts could be due to the introduction of appropriate extrinsic feedback (1). Either feedback is withdrawn for attempts 6 and 7 or it is inappropriate, for example, relying on intrinsic feedback from the performer. Alternatively, at this point the performer had reached their peak without time for further practice (1). Attempts 8 and 9 show a further increase in success; this could be due to the performer developing intrinsic feedback, learning from their own mistakes (1).

76. The inverted-U theory
To get full marks, you need to: draw the shape of the curve correctly (1); correctly label each axis (1).

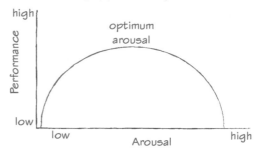

77. Stress management 1
For the high jumper, mental rehearsal is going through the phases of the run up and jump in his mind (1). This will help him mentally prepare, focusing solely on the jump and nothing else (1). This will build his confidence, as he sees himself successfully clearing the bar (1).

78. Stress management 2
They might say, "Come on, relax, you have saved penalties from this team before, you can do it again" (1).

79. Aggression
indirect aggression (1)

80. Personality
Introverts tend to be shy (1), therefore prefer activities where they can be thoughtful and work on their own; archery allows them to do this (1). Introverts also prefer sports requiring precision (1); archery is a very precise sport, requiring fine skills to hit the target, rather than the gross skills needed in team sports, for example when tackling in rugby (1).

81. Motivation
An elite footballer will receive extrinsic, tangible rewards (1), for example medals or trophies if they win a tournament (1). They will also receive extrinsic, intangible rewards (1), for example the fame associated with being elite (1).

Socio-cultural influences

82. Social groups: family, friends and peers
Brooklyn is influenced by his family (1). As his Dad is a professional footballer, Brooklyn would have been introduced to football when he was young and has continued playing it (1).

83. Gender and age
Factor 1: Accessibility (1). If you are under the legal driving age you may be reliant on public transport or others to take you to play sport (if the club is not within walking distance) (1).

Factor 2: Disposable income (1). If you are still at school you may not be able to afford to play sport (1).

84. Race/religion/culture and disability
Paul might face lack of access (1), as there might not be anywheelchair basketball clubs in the area (1).

85. Commercialisation
Commercial organisations are interested in sponsoring events such as the Olympic Games because they get huge audiences (1), therefore increasing the number of people worldwide that will see the organisation's product and want to buy or use it (1).

86. The advantages of commercialisation
Their product will be associated with one of the best performer in the sport (1), therefore fans will think the product is good and want to buy it (1).

87. The disadvantages of commercialisation
The company is associated with Armstrong's cheating (1), therefore the sponsors' products are no longer as popular (1) and sales of them will go down (1).

88. The advantages of technology
The advances in wheelchair technology mean that the wheelchair will be more manoeuvrable (1), so that the player can move freely about the court (1).

89. The disadvantages of technology
The technology is expensive to install (1), therefore money will be spent on this rather than on other facilities, equipment or even grassroots (1) that could be used to improve performance of current or future players in the sport (1).

90. Conduct of performers
sportsmanship (1)

91. Blood doping
The athlete's blood can become contaminated during storage or preparation for re-injection (1). If the contaminated blood is re-injected it will cause infection (1).

92. Beta blockers
They have a calming effect, allowing the heart rate to slow down (1).

93. Stimulants
If a performer has had a long season and is tired (1) but needs to be alert for a big event, then they may take stimulants (1).

94. Narcotic analgesics
Narcotic analgesics (1)

95. Anabolic agents
Example answer:
Liver damage (1), testicular atrophy (1)

96. Diuretics
C: Diuretics (1)

97. Peptide hormones
EPO increases red blood cell count (1), which means the runner will be able to carry more oxygen (1). This means they can maintain a good energy supply throughout the race, allowing them to maintain a better pace and run the distance more quickly (1).

98. Pros and cons of taking PEDs
An elite performer might take performance-enhancing drugs because they desperately want to win (1) so they can get better sponsorship deals (1).

99. Spectator behaviour
Example answer:
Spectators can create a positive atmosphere in a stadium (1). This can motivate the players to work hard, making the game more exciting to watch (1).

Health, fitness and well-being

100. Physical health and fitness
An example of poor physical health is obesity (1). This would make it harder to run in sporting activities owing to additional body fat (1), meaning the performer could not run very fast or for very long (1).

101. Mental (emotional) health
If you play sport you will want to win, but will not always do so which can be frustrating (1). Playing sport therefore gives you the opportunity to practise controlling your emotions and to realise that you can play well even if you don't win (1). This increases your confidence, as you begin to feel better about yourself (1).

102. Social health
A social benefit of participation is increased cooperation (1). If you can work with others without arguing (a social benefit), this will increase enjoyment (an emotional benefit) (1).

103. Sedentary lifestyle
Driving to work rather than cycling (1) can lead to excessive weight gain (1) as a result of burning fewer calories through inactivity (1).

104. Obesity
1 Example answer: Heart disease (1); type 2 diabetes (1)
2 By having more body fat than you should you are making your body work harder (1), therefore energy supply will deplete sooner, making it difficult to participate in physical activity (1). This will mean fitness cannot increase, so the individual is less likely to be motivated to sustain involvement in physical activity (1).

105. Somatotypes: mesomorphs
1 A mesomorph body type could increase muscle mass for more power, so that the tennis player could make the ball travel faster, making it harder to return (1).
2 Rugby (1)

106. Somatotypes: ectomorphs and endomorphs

1 An endormorph body type would be an advantage in events where additional weight makes it harder for your opposition, such as some positions in rugby, or sumo wrestling (1).

2 They would be much heavier than someone with an ectomorph body type, so their performance would deteriorate (1). This is because they would be carrying excess body weight (1), therefore slowing them down (1).

107. Balanced diet and energy use

Men are generally larger than women and therefore require a higher calorie intake (1); also fewer calories are required as you age owing to a slower metabolism (1).

108. Nutrition

B: Minerals (1)

109. Water balance

1 Dehydration is excessive loss of body water interrupting the function of the body (1).

2 Example answer:
Otherwise they will suffer with muscle fatigue and their performance will drop (1).

Paper 2 Extended answer questions

Marks are awarded for the depth and breadth of knowledge demonstrated about the question topics, the application of this knowledge to the context of the question, and the level of evaluation made. The use of appropriate essay format and correct terminology in a structured and coherent way is also taken in to consideration when awarding credit.

110. Paper 2 – Extended answer question 1

The inverted-U theory states that as arousal increases so does performance up to an optimum point after which, if arousal continues to rise, performance will drop owing to the performer becoming over anxious. Therefore it is important that the performer stays at the optimum level of arousal, to make sure their performance does not drop. However, different activities, or different skills and techniques within an activity, will have different optimum arousal levels. For example, an archer will require a lower level of arousal to perform his/her sport than a boxer will; similarly, a striker taking a penalty in football will need a lower level of arousal than during normal play, so that he/she can focus on taking the penalty.

A golf putt is another example of a skill that requires a lower level of arousal. This is because it is a fine skill, compared to a tackle in rugby, which is a gross skill and therefore requires a higher level of arousal for the performer to play at their best. The level of skill will also affect the optimum level of arousal, for example a beginner will need a lower level of arousal than an expert, even if they are playing the same game or performing the same skill.

111. Paper 2 – Extended answer question 2

There are different types of guidance: visual, verbal, manual and mechanical.

Visual guidance is where the performer is shown the skill being completed correctly so that they can see how it should look and then copy it. Frankie's coach could demonstrate the back somersault or ask someone else who was good at them to demonstrate. This type of guidance is very useful with beginners, as this helps them to develop a mental image of the skill they need to perform.

Verbal guidance is when the coach gives teaching points. For example, they may shout 'hips forward and up' to remind Frankie about that part of the technique. However, this is only any good if Frankie knows what this means. As he is a beginner at this skill, he is unlikely to understand and therefore will not do the technique correctly, which is likely to result in injury. To help avoid injury the coach could use either manual or mechanical guidance.

In manual guidance the coach would physically support Frankie to complete the move to help him get the correct feel of the movement while feeling supported. For difficult skills such as somersaults, mechanical guidance would be used. This would probably be via a harness so that, if Frankie does the skill incorrectly, the coach can stop Frankie crashing to the trampoline. This reduces the chance of injury and will increase Frankie's confidence before attempting the move without support. Even though this would be the best method of guidance, the coach needs to be careful not to let Frankie become too reliant on it. If he does, it will be difficult psychologically for Frankie to attempt the move without the harness.

Notes

Notes

Published by Pearson Education Limited, 80 Strand, London, WC2R 0RL.
www.pearsonschoolsandfecolleges.co.uk

Text and illustrations © Pearson Education Ltd 2018
Typeset and illustrated by Kamae Design, Oxford
Produced by Out of House Publishing
Cover illustration by Eoin Coveney

The right of Jan Simister to be identified as author of this work has been asserted by her
in accordance with the Copyright, Designs and Patents Act 1988.

First published 2018
21
10 9 8 7 6

British Library Cataloguing in Publication Data
A catalogue record for this book is available from the British Library

ISBN 978 1 292 20484 0

Acknowledgements
The authors and publisher would like to thank the following individuals and organisations for
their kind permission to reproduce copyright material.

Page 101 'Mental health: a state of well-being' http://www.who.int/features/factfiles/mental_
health/en/. August 2014; page 118 Used with the permission of the World Anti-Doping Agency
(WADA) and may not be reproduced or otherwise cited without the express permission of
WADA; page 120 'Constitution of WHO: principles', http://www.who.int/about/mission/en/;
page 120 'Mental health: a state of well-being', http://www.who.int/features/factfiles/mental_
health/en/. August 2014; pages 118–124 AQA material is reproduced by permission of AQA.

Photographs
(Key: b-bottom; c-centre; l-left; r-right; t-top)

123RF: Magiceyes 26; **Alamy Stock Photo**: Split Seconds 11b, Yon Marsh 42, Allstar Picture
Library 82l, Neil Tingle 88l, 89b; **Corbis**: Robert Michael 28b; **Getty Images**: Fuse/Corbis 2b,
Technotr/Vetta 7, Matthew Stockman 9, Ian Walton 25b, Mark Ralston/AFP 31tl, Al Bello
34r, Laurence Griffiths 36cr, George Doyle/Stockbyte 48r, Hero Images 77t, Ty Allison 77b,
Lars Baron 86, David Munden/Popperfoto 90tr, Sandra Behne/Bongarts 90b, Patrik Giardino/
Corbis 95l, Mike Powell/Allsport Concepts 97r, Anadolu Agency 99b; **Glow Images**: Image
100/Corbis 13tl, 92; **Imagestate**: John Foxx Collection 90tl; **Pearson Education Australia Pvt
Ltd**: 57l, 57r; **Rex Features**: Ian Hodgson/ANL 82r; **Science Photo Library**: D. Roberts 2t;
Shutterstock: Alex Mit 1t, 15, Mitzy 1b, Debby Wong 6, Jiang Dao Hua 8t, 34l, Dotshock 8b,
81b, Stephen Mcsweeny 10, 28c, Pete Saloutos 11t, Galina Barskaya 12, Eugene Onischenko
13tr, CLS Digital Arts 13b, Carlos E. Santa Maria 14t, Air Images 14c, Tankist276 14b, 40b,
Denis Kuvaev 23t, Pajtica 23b, Peter Bernik 24, 112, Olena Yakobchuk 55tl, 64, Rido 25t, 109t,
Paolo Bona 27, 78r, Maxisport 28tl, 79b, Nicholas Piccillo 28tr, 46, Ronald Sumners 29, Stocky
Images 31tr, John Lumb 31b, 36t, Samuel Borges Photography 32, Mitch Gunn 33l, 79t, Inge
Schepers 33r, Snap2Art 36cl, Racheal Grazias 36b, Corepics VOF 37l, Ljupco Smokovski 37r,
Chaoss 38t, Mike Orlov 38b, Stefan Schurr 39t, Lilyana Vynogradova 40t, Orange Line Media
48l, Diego Cervo 48c, Andreja Donko 52, Ramon Espelt Photography 55tr, Wavebreakmedia
55tc, 74b, Muratart 55b, Andrey Yurlov 61, Monkey Business Images 63, 80c, Undrey 74t,
Carlos Caetano 78l, 80br, Frank Wasserfuehrer 79c, Mezzotint 80t, Chen WS 80bl, lzf 81tl,
Sondem 81tr, Roomanald 83, Padmayogini 85, Karin Hildebrand Lau 87, 101Akarca 88r, Iurii
Osadchi 89t, Lisa S. 91l, Nils Z 91r, Aleksandar Todorovic 95r, Mikhail Pogosov 96, Stefan
Holm 97l, Evlakhov Valeriy 98, Ververidis Vasilis 99t, Rob Marmion 100, Creativa Images 104,
Valeriy Velikov 105, Sirtravelalot 106, Rob van Esch 109b, Xixinxing 117; **Sozaijiten**: 8c, 39b

All other images © Pearson Education

Note from the publisher
Pearson has robust editorial processes, including answer and fact checks, to ensure the
accuracy of the content in this publication, and every effort is made to ensure this publication
is free of errors. We are, however, only human, and occasionally errors do occur. Pearson is
not liable for any misunderstandings that arise as a result of errors in this publication, but it is
our priority to ensure that the content is accurate. If you spot an error, please do contact us at
resourcescorrections@pearson.com so we can make sure it is corrected.